ALASKA
THE GREAT BEAR'S CUB

Let us probe the silent places, let us see what
    luck betide us;
Let us journey to a lonely land I know.
There's a whisper on the night wind, there's a
    star agleam to guide us,
And the wind is calling, calling . . . let us
    go.

ROBERT SERVICE.

MARY LEE DAVIS WEARS AN ESKIMO PARKA OF MUSKRAT AND WOL-
VERINE, REINDEER MUKLUKS AND SIBERIAN MITTENS.

ALASKA
The Great Bear's Cub

By
MARY LEE DAVIS
*Author of " Uncle Sam's Attic, The Intimate
Story of Alaska "*

ILLUSTRATED BY PEN AND INK ILLUSTRATIONS BY
OLAUS JOHAN MURIE AND AUTHOR'S PHOTOGRAPHS

W. A. WILDE COMPANY
PUBLISHERS   BOSTON

Made in United States of America

CONTENTS

7

8 CONTENTS

ILLUSTRATIONS

9

ALASKA
The Great Bear's Cub

I

The Untamed of Diomedes

Oppress not the cubs of the strangers, but hail
them as Sisters and Brothers.
For though they are little and fubsy, it may be
The Bear is their mother.
KIPLING.

MAPS make a picture to me, as perhaps they do to you—strange shapes, as people often guess at cloud forms and see twisting dragons or a battlemented castle there, some dream thing hatched from memory or imagining. Alaska's map is such a picture to my mind, perhaps fantastical. But I, who've lived there long, see often with a flash of vividness a strangely moving picture, whenever on a flickering memory screen that outline of America's High North is thrown in profile.

Years ago, in the Bad Lands of Wyoming, I caught a glimpse of something few can see, these days of lost frontiers. I saw two wild stallions fighting.

It was at a water-hole near which our survey party camped in a summer of little rain. Lying upon the ground and using strong field-glasses, which brought things close so that I seemed almost to touch, I watched two groups of renegade and outlaw horses approach the trampled spring, with caution and with prick-eared care—and with suspicion, too, for this was closer to the hated taint of men than they had come in many moons. Weeks of a great drought forced them from the inner hills, and water must be had.

Then, as one bunch of mares drank and their master stood on guard, the other wild-eyed, ragged horse-group came down from the opposite mesas, emerging from a twisted Bad Land coulée. The startled mares lifted their heads, wheeled, circled and retreated from the trampled water, a swirl of mane and tail and flying color—then turned and faced about in semicircle. The two opposing crested stallions, after shrill cries of challenge, stepped out stiffly erect, walking with collected careful menace. They seemed to bristle as dogs do who meet, for the tossed manes were tumbled on arched necks, heads very high, nostrils outstretched, their long and flowing tails held at stiff horizontal. Their fore-feet seemed but lightly to touch the hard baked earth, in that slow coming on, which was as ominous and formal as preparation for a duel.

Then, as they met, they reared, and fought— and were no longer horses, as I who had long loved and broken horses knew the breed. They were possessed demonic wild beasts, that screamed and tore and plunged and thrust sharp-pointed hoofs of horn that cut the flesh and laid great bleeding gashes open. Their loud high screams were unlike any horse cry I had ever known— more horrid, even, than that agonizing sound of burning horses trapped in barn-fire. Curling far-back-drawn lips bared yellow teeth, that ripped and tore. They clinched in mid-air, bore down on each other with the berserk fury of grim savage wrestlers—and struck and struck and struck again, with bared fang and with slashing hoof, the while two groups of huddled mares stood stiffly quiet, tense and alert, unmoving yet not unmoved.

Such fury could not be for long, and when the smaller stallion—his neck laid open in a horrid wound, his fore leg broken—dragged himself finally aside, the faithless mares answered the loud neigh of the champion, crossed over with a dainty pace and only look of scorn for their once master. One or two squealed with an affected fright and scampered past the taint of blood, while others merely swerved aside as they passed by, like dainty ladies withdrawing from something not quite " nice." With the proud horse-thing leading, they trailed behind him up the gulch, and soon the muddied water-hole between the red-baked hills was quiet again, blazingly sun drenched, silent.

From those Wyoming Bad Lands and from Colorado's mining camps, I went to far Interior Alaska. For many years the outline of the new country, unlike the outline of so many other lands, refused to lend itself to picture making. It seemed so curious a shape that it intrigued my fancy, but nothing seemed to fit its contour. There was that long extended southeast strip, beginning just at 54° 40′ (a fighting number that!) and stretching long miles up and out to Sitka, Skagway and Mount Saint Elias. There was the great bulk of the wide strong land, almost a continent itself, rearing into the very North until it pricked the paleocrystic sea at Barrow. There was the out-thrust of the Alaska Peninsula, moving fiery and molten, and the long curving stretch of the outflung Aleutians, reaching to strike at Asia. And up above the Pribilofs, Nunivak, St. Lawrence, Nome, rose Seward Peninsula, like a monster head, jutting far westward at Cape

Prince of Wales until it all but breathed upon and touched Siberia.

What creature was this shape—this strange Alaska which plunged so fearlessly out from one continent, to challenge yet another older land?

I sailed along the southeast coast and up behind the mountainy islands; I lived for years within the body of the land, right at its heart; I drifted down the length of Yukon and out to Bering Sea, St. Michael, Nome, and north to Teller, Lost River and the Asia-facing cape. I saw the little islands that lie like stepping stones between the massy continents, and I asked their name. And when men said, " The Diomedes," I knew the picture puzzle had been solved.

Diomedes, Thracian king, whose swift and fearful steeds lived upon flesh: Diomedes, whose horses only Hercules could capture—Hercules, " stronger than everything except his own passion! " Beautiful and wild, with power unharnessed, spirit untamed, strength unguessed, mettle and fruitfulness yet unexploited—this was the picture which the land's map reared for me into the High North, the untamed thing whose taming must remain a work for Hector or eighth toil for Hercules.

The map-picture is a great horse, rearing. Firm hind hooves rest a major weight upon the warm earth of the continent, solidly planted there in earliest settlements and growing pioneer cities. Long legs, well sinewed, stretch up from Ketchikan to Juneau. That firm well-barreled and deep-chested body rears out in a tremendous energetic arch of leaping line until flame-tipped volcanic-crusted fore-hooves strike, plunging out across the northern sea to Asia, Kuriles and Kamchatka, where the Aleutians splash the North Pacific. That up-flung broad-browed head of Seward Peninsula reaches an open nostril to sniff Siberian air and neigh a challenge to a half-forgotten Russian sire. Frost-crested mane flows up and back and out into the very Arctic. Here was a picture made—as pictures are—from fact and memory and fancy: Alaskan sketch drawn from that water-hole of distant *Mauvaises Terres,* fantastic, as star-gazing Ancients drew great pictured beasts out of the upper skies and etched their constellations out of star points—Taurus and Leo and the Great and Little Bear—half real and half a notion in men's minds.

A constellation in the Northern skies! Here was another thought to play with. In shape, this land in very truth was plunging horse; but in its temper (as I so well had come, by then, to know it) and in heredity and place upon earth's globe,

it was assuredly the Great Bear's cub, son of
Ursa Major, born under that Lode Star which
has forever drawn the wandering and adventuring. And it was son, too, of the great and hulk-
ing Russian Bear that lived so near by 'cross the
narrow straits—the Bear that walks like Man.
To understand Alaska you should know bears.
No creature is more characteristic of Alaska, no
animal is seen there in a greater variety—almost
the fabled fifty-seven, I believe, for there are
white and brown bears, grizzlies, Kodiaks, glaciers, cinnamon and silver tips, with all the inter-
vening intermediary crosses. And Alaska has
the patience of the bear, his curiosity and his rustling resource, his caution and his playfulness, as
well as the great teachability which is the bear
cub's heritage, together with the strength which
comes through long and brooding hibernation.
Secure within his homeland North, this cub of
the Great Bear rests here under Polaris, knowing
his star of destiny, knowing the whence and
whither of those ursine constellations that swing
and wheel through the successive equinoxes.

If you know bears, then you will understand
the mettle of Alaska. Thirteen cub colonies upon
another then-distant northern continental coast
were lion whelps; and you can't know much of
America's youth unless you know something, at

least, of the British Lion's ways. Alaska is an unlicked bear cub, young and half-grown and wild yet, though in first cub-hood the Russians put an iron ring in his nose and made him dance to a rough music. In spirit and in tempo of his life, the land is Ursus arctos, lacking the nervous energy of that prancing horse, lacking its swift speed, but with an even greater though a very different strength: abiding time, living on the land, on catch of berries, salmon, mushrooms, all the varied richness spread upon his northern mountain shelves, through which he ranges so securely. Withdrawn into his hills in winter, protected by the snows, living with the sun and round the sun, tuned to the zodiacal year, tremendous, forceful, young, untamed—Alaska, Cub of the Great Bear.

Think of Alaska, then, in shape as a strong plunging horse, out-reared toward Asia. But if you wish to catch the symbol and the mystery of that Russian-North heredity which enters so much of Alaskan life and temper, then think in terms of Ursus arctos and remember that the land is young and new, wild yet in many ways and shy of strangers. Then you will surely catch a glimpse of whence and whither, in the High North of To-day.

If you are not grown up, then come to Alaska

with me. For only those whose hearts are young
(no matter what the tell-tale family Bible may
tattle about birth dates) go North with genuine
happiness. It's young hearts for adventure, and
the hard work that always waits on true adventure but which is afterward forgotten. Of course,
I was rather young myself when I first went to
Alaska. Yet even now I can say truly (and this
is in the nature of a confession!) I've seldom
seen a real grown-up, even in my own mirror!

Alaska is so very young, to-day, that it is of
most interest to those who think in a big way of
futures. Only those who have far-sighted eyes,
only those with forward-looking faces, only those
whose feet itch for the touch of trails unblazed
and soil unbroken, will glory in The North.
Alaska has appealed to Captain John Smith and
Sir Walter Raleigh types of mind, to John Rolfe
and Miles Standish types. Alaska has appealed
to people like Ben Eielson and Sir Hubert Wilkins, Amundsen and Stefansson. It's not a place
for hide-bound minds of any stripe. It is a fu-
ture-looking land on the world's rim, facing the
Far East; and only those turn to it happily
whose faces are set toward those far horizons, the
frontiers of to-morrow.

Here is the yet remaining American sanctuary
for those who love American wilderness: a land

for out-of-doors people, a land of newness and of breadth and clean spaces, and the life of the wild. Red-skinned indigenes are here, as well as mongoloid Eskimos whose sloe eyes speak of near-by Asia. And Russian names and ways haunt this Alaska, too, from the days out of the bristling darkness of a not-far past when those great sentimental comedians, Peter, Elizabeth and Catherine " played their Tsarships," in Shaw's phrase, " as eccentric character parts and produced scene after scene of furious harlequinade, with the monarch as clown." There are no city brick-scapes here, but many rugged virile villages of the always new frontier. Alaska's men are addicted to mackinaw, parka and shoe-pac rather than to swallowtail and striped trouser-leg. Their minds are rich in swirling splendid nebular ideas, stardust from which new worlds of fact are ever being born. Their dreams are high, wide dreams of future empire. Their hands are calloused and their ears a-ring to stroke of ax blazing new ways for state-craft to come and follow wood-craft, fur-craft, fish-craft—the ancient pioneer way in the unbroken North. Nor is this any strange and alien land, but integral part and bone both of our American continent and our American nation: a land sadly mis-prized, a land much misunderstood, for it is not an Ice Land but a Green Land,

a land of paradoxical wheat and heat quite as
much as a land of gold and cold.

Young yet, wild yet, its youth and wildness are
the very facts which make for strength, solicit
solitude, and promise plenty.   Its beauty is untamed, its people wind-blown pollen, its wild life
taunts and haunts, its land-ways and its water-
paths and air-trails call and beckon.   It is the
land of great expectation, yet to be fulfilled.
The pen that writes its history has but recently
been dipped in ink.   The story is yet new.   And
yet it has already called to Russian Cossack and
to great James Cook, to Argonauts of '98 seeking a golden fleece, to trapper, hunter, mountain
climber and explorer—to all whose interest's on
the ragged edge of mystery, novelty and adventure.   And these hyperboreans have plucked the
blue flower here of happiness, even from the rim
of the Polar Sea.   With true and exquisite ap-
propriateness, forget-me-not is this land's em-
blem.

Those whose hearts are young (and our Alaska
will know no others) find here not only America's last and lost frontier but a true friend in
the truly friendly Arctic.   That friend (whom I
went far to seek, I lived with long, to whom my
heart all ways returns) I ask you to come with
me and also know.   Robert Service wrote un-

forgettably of the Spell of the Yukon.   The Yukon, that great roadway of the North, has nowise
lost its haunting spell, to-day.

> " Walk lightly,
>   Hands upon your eyes;
>   For he who looks on wild earth *once*
>   Looks until he dies."

II

54° 40' and Metlakatla

Ye whose hearts are fresh and simple,
Who have faith in God and Nature,
Who believe that in all ages
Every human heart is human;
That in even savage bosoms
There are longings, yearnings, strivings
For the good they comprehend not;
That the feeble hands and helpless,
Groping blindly in the darkness,
Touch God's right hand in that darkness
And are lifted up and strengthened;—
Listen to this simple story.

LONGFELLOW.

FOR years I have been hoping to meet the woman who was my geography teacher in grade school, for there is something I wish mightily to tell her. Something she taught me once, I've since found out is not *exactly* true! She thought it was, for people used to know so little of Alaska then and old geographies pictured a land of snow and ice—which makes us smile who live here, for you should see our riotous summer gardens of flowers and vegetables. She taught me (and that was what the school books all said, then): " Alaska is a land of Eskimos."

23

Since I've been living here, I've found that statement just one quarter true. One quarter of the people in Alaska are Eskimos, they live in only one quarter of Alaska, and there are many other Eskimo people who do not live in Alaska at all, but elsewhere: in Siberia, in the Mackenzie country and Hudson Bay region of Canada, and even far over east in Greenland. After I had lived in Alaska for some time, I came to have a very dear Eskimo friend, who told me much about her people; and when I went to Nome one summer, the capital of Alaska's really Eskimo country, I met through her great numbers of her kinsmen and myself learned much of their pleasant ways and manners.

But that's a later story. I mention it here only because when most people go to Alaska and think at all about Alaska, Eskimos come to mind, first, last and always, I believe; and most people are surprised (as I know I was) to find that the Natives of the greater portion of Alaska (all of that portion lying along the southern coast and well into the Interior) are Indians, and not Eskimos at all. When I went North first, the officers on the boat were highly amused because, when we neared 54° 40' and the southern boundary of Alaska, I began to ask about Eskimos. The jolly old captain had been answering my many questions patiently, for he knew that I was not merely curious but really wanted to know, since I was going North to live.

"Why, I've been navigating these south-eastern Alaska waters, man and boy," he said, "for more years than I'll tell you. And, bless me, ma'am, I don't believe I've *ever* laid my eye on a full-blooded Eskimo. No sir, I don't know, as I have. There's plenty of them further north, and nice folks, too, I'm told, by men who've lived amongst them. Most people, like yourself, expect to see Eskimos as soon as ever we cross the line here. I guess the teachin' books must some of 'em have been written long ago, when many folks didn't travel this-a-way. People ought to know better than to ask to find Eskimos—who're a north-loving people, so I'm told, and can't abide mild weather—here along this south coast where the Japan Current (Black Stream, *we* call it) and the warmish wind that's mate to it, soften the air and moist it, year around, same as you see to-day.

"Why, ma'am, this part here has a climate just like Seattle or Washington, D. C., or certain shires I know in England, every moon of the calendar, too, and for the selfsame reason. Climates come up from the sea, good part, as we seafaring men best know; and a warm sea beats on these islands and these coasts round here, and makes 'em no fit place for Eskimos. Why, ma'am, they'd perish of the sweat, in those thick tight fur coats of theirs I've seen in pictures, if they lived in *these* latitudes. No, ma'am, I can't show you Eskimos on *this* run. But with each rung of the ladder as you hitch further north on this course, some things grow curiouser and curiouser. And you'll find one of the *most* curious right here at 54° 40′ if you'll keep your eyes open —just beyond Prince Rupert on Annette Island, at Metlakatla.

" Here's the most interestin' crew of Indians ever *I* heard tell of, yet folks who travel don't seem to know much of anything about 'em. I've known Indians, forever, seems how, for I came to this coast when I was neither man nor boy but something in between 'em both! And what these Natives here have done and still do, looks to me like a prize sample of the way a crowd of Indians —if they want to tie up by themselves, I mean— can be jo-mighty independent and happy.

" As I said, all of this Alaska you are headed for, except that northmost part where the real Eskimos live, is the home of Indians, of several tribes, quite a distinct lot. Now the Indians at Metlakatla are Tsimpseans, something less than a thousand of them; but unlike most other Alaska

Indians they have stuck together, have their own
Native minister, their own town meeting, stores,
a cooperage, run a fish cannery that pays good
royalties, raise fine gardens, and have a peach of
a band that sure can play good lively tunes, for
they're just *full* of music! They dress and act
like white folks, manage everything on the island,
and are one of the most up and doing *tribes* of
Indians in America. The queer thing is, it's all
the work of one man, really. They are a mighty
peculiar people, and no one but a queer duck like
old Father Duncan would have stuck with 'em
so long and made anything out of 'em, I reckon.
One fellow called him an Apostle to Alaska. He
was an ' apostle ' all right, but not to Alaska,
just to Metlakatla. All he ever saw or knew of
the Territory was just this little south tip-end of
it, and any work of his that lasted was bounded
by this small island. But he knew Metlakatla,
all right, and he's the man who put it on the map.
For Metlakatla *is* Father Duncan.

" And say, you ought to know about that chap.
Back in the middle of last century, whalers and
explorers and navy men going back home to England from this country, told how the Indians were
ill treated by the Hudson Bay outfit, who had a
fort just back behind there, in British Columbia,
and were about the only white folks nearabouts,

those days. Fort Simpson was a place all built
around with heavy palisades, some thirty feet
high, made of thick trunks of trees driven into
the ground and riveted together. It had a heavy
double gate bound with iron, and there were four
big corner bastions, and galleries with cannon
mounted in them that meant business, let *me* tell
you, and sentinels on duty night and day. That's
how *they* felt toward Indians, don't you see?
They hated and mistrusted them, and just were
here to do them out of furs and things, it looked
like. Only a few bucks at a time were ever let
inside the fort, to trade. Hudson Bay thought
the Natives were a bad lot—and what the Natives
thought about the Hudson Bay doings, don't get
itself printed!

"Well, William Duncan heard about all this,
and it didn't listen good to him, *a*-tall. He happened to be one of those really Christian-minded
fellows, who couldn't bear to think of under-dogs
getting a dirty deal. He gave up a right good
job he had, in a wholesale leather house back
home, and packed out here all the ways round the
Horn, to this Fort Simpson. He picked him up
a Native buck—named Clah—for teacher, and
pitched right in to learn the lingo. And lots more
than the lingo, too, for Duncan was a wise and
canny Yorkshireman, and he saw right off that

he had to learn the way the Indian *mind* worked, or he'd never get himself inside it. And that is what he set himself to do. Yes sir, and he did it, too. One fellow here said of him that he crawled into their very thoughts, like Indian hunters stalk their game!

" So, before Father Duncan, as they came to call him, ever began to preach at all, he learned their talk from bottom up. You know right well, ma'am, if you're clumsy in a language, you can offend folks terrible without meaning to *a*-tall. And he was bound that he would hurt no feelings.

" And now just let me tell you, learning *their* talk is a he-man job, for it's as queer-contraped language as ever you set tongue into! The Hudson Bay crowd never even tried it. They had a sort of pidgin-English called Chinook, used for trade all up and down the coast, and that did *them*. But that wa'n't Duncan's way. No sir, he wa'n't any chap to compromise or go by halves. Stiff hearted, that's what the old codger was, and all for setting full sail on a straight course and letting her drive.

" This Tsimpsean lingo I was telling you about —why, they have five different words for every blessed *number* on the chart! What do you know about that? Yes sir, and different for talking

about different *kinds* of things. I never did hear
anything just like it. I used to do some trading
on my own, up and down the coast here, and I
picked up some of it, for you have to know your
numbers in a dicker! Take ' *two,*' for instance.
If it was something flat you asked about, like
blankets, then ' two ' was *topral;* but if it was
round things like dollars, ' two ' was something
else again, *kapal.* Two men or two women would
be *tupahdool.* As if that wa'n't enough, two
canoes was something else again, a word that
sounded like *kalbailk;* but for any long narrow
thing they had two of, the word was *koapskan.*
Now, can you imagine any white man wanting
to learn a lingo like that? You've got to hand it
to Duncan, for he did it.

" Why, they had words ten and twelve syllables long, for *lots* of things, too—regular jaw
breakers, I call 'em. And another funny thing
about their talk: if it was *one* thing you wanted to
call ' nice ' or ' bad ' or ' big ' or any other name,
it would be *one* parcel of words; but if there were
two of them—say, did they fit a letter ' s ' on to
the stern of those same words, good and shipshape, like white folks do? No sir, nothing so
plain sailing as that. They had a whole *other set*
of words to call the plurals of things by. Now,
can you beat it? It's a kind of talk would drive

you to the mad-house, learning, I'd say. And this queer codger Duncan had to get it all from young Clah, his Native boy who didn't know one word of English. And all they had in common to lay a course by was this Chinook trade talk, which wa'n't so long on friendly words or Sunday School expressions, let *me* tell you! The early traders didn't talk one bit pretty. They carried more hard words than soft in their cargo! It's small wonder those Canadian Tsimpseans had no word at all for ' thank you ' in their language, while the very commonest word in Thlingit, further north, is ' thanks,' *goo-nulth-cheesh.*

" But old Duncan did it. Yes sir, and he wa'n't a minister and he wa'n't a priest, neither. He was just a plain Christian man, set on doing these strange people here some good. He had his enemies, for he wa'n't the easiest one in all the world to get on with. But he had a great way with him, and even his worst enemies never denied his doing heaps of good here.

" Well, as I said, he learned the talk from bottom up. But first he started soap making.

" Yes sir, you'd think that soap would be about the last thing ever Indians hankered for. But they *loved* soap, and Hudson Bay had charged them four fine sable skins or fifty mink skins for one finger-thick cake of it! Now, that *was* rather

steep. And when this Duncan fellow showed
them how to make soap for themselves—from
oolakan grease, a sort of candle-fish they caught
near by—they were so tickled that they took him
right on as first mate, and for the rest of that
cruise he sure did have the edge!

"But did the Hudson Bay people like this?
I'll say they didn't. They saw profits slipping,
sure, and made things hot for Duncan, right
away—and Hudson Bay was just about al-
mighty, then, all up and down this coast. So
Father Duncan pulled up stakes, one rainy day;
but some fifty Indians followed him, to a new
camp they'd made. And the next fortnight, what
do you suppose? Why, in around the bend came
thirty great big war canoes, all loaded to the line
with Indians—three hundred of them—all come
to live with Father Duncan and learn some more,
they said, about ' the good ways.'

"They made their final set-up at Metlakatla, a
word that means ' an inlet with an outlet,' just
over the line here on American soil. An old
Tongass Thlingit village it had been, burned out
in one of their wars. Hoisted a U. S. flag, they
did—' the flag of the Boston men ' *they* called it,
because they'd seen it first on old-time U. S.
whaling vessels—and formally transferred themselves from Johnny Bull to Uncle Samuel. They

called this queer old bachelor boss of theirs by a word that means ' chief,' in their lingo; and he was that all right, a managin' man, an autocrat, if ever there was one. Wouldn't let 'em even whistle or run, of a Sunday. No sir, though now he's gone they've got more careless, like the rest of us! But he had some nifty notions about this self-governin' idea, too, something like our Founding Fathers. So he rigged up a sort of town council for his Natives, elected true and shipshape and in good old town-meetin' style; and made them a police force, and laid out taxes of so many blankets, per, for ' public works.'

"He had a sharp eye for hides, too, being's how he'd worked in that leather house back home. So naturally he'd kept his ear open about fur prices, and such—the Hudson Bay's big play, here. When he got settled in the new place, right off he rigged up a fur-trade on his own, and he sure got the business. For where the Hudson Bay had paid ' Lo,' the poor Indian, two bits (that's Alaska for a quarter, ma'am) for a mar- ten skin—what you ladies call a ' sable '—old Father Duncan paid from two to four dollars, depending on the color, grading up if the pelt really was a black or ' sable.' For he'd made in- quiry and knew what he could sell 'em for Out- side, as we Alaskans call The States. Being a

Yorkshireman, you can just bet he didn't lose
any money, even at that! And where The Company had paid all of two copper Indian cents
(one British penny, mind) for mink pelts, the
old boy bought 'em up over *his* counter for four
to six bits; and sea otter (which the Russians and
the Canton trade set such a heap of store by),
where Hudson Bay paid ten or twelve dollars
for one of those fine skins (Ever see one, ma'am?
'Tis likely not, for the old traders hunted 'em so
hard, they're nearly all gone, now)—why, Duncan planked out a good hundred bucks for one,
when *his* Natives fetched 'em in to him.

"Well sir, of course the Hudson Bay were
plumb set against this nonsense, of paying natives what the fur-catch was really worth. They
wouldn't fetch the Tsimpseans any outfit after
this move—flat refused to haul freight to Metlakatla. Freeze the old man out, they would. So
Father Duncan up and bought a schooner for
himself, and his Indians all bought ' shares ' in
it, just as he told 'em to, and they had a Native
master for her and a Native crew. Good seamen,
too, these fellows. And when their big tyee
(Duncan, I mean) called a great wa-wa and the
profits from that first year's trading were
whacked up, all fair and square, and Father Duncan, gruff old gaffer but well meanin', explained

just how their profits had been made—say, you
can bet a great light dawned right then.

"Well sir, they've kept it up, they have—co-
operative notions all down the line; and when
their dividend day came round and profits were
cut up and handed out, the old men wagged their
heads and said, 'The *blankets* have grown big!'
One time, when Father Duncan had got some
cash from somewheres and rigged them up a tidy
sawmill, I've heard that one old Native came to
him and said, '*Shimauget* (that's their word for
chief, and what the old men always called him)—
Shimauget, now I want to die.'

"Well sir, the little Yorkshire chief was sure
flabbergasted.

"'For why?' he wants to know.

"'I want to be first man, tell dead chiefs,' the
Native said, 'how now us Tsimpseans *make the
water cut the wood!*'

"Since Father Duncan died, not so long since,
the U. S. acts as sort of grand-daddy to 'em; and
their being the only reservation Indians in
Alaska, the other Natives sort of feel that Uncle
Sam has made pets of these 'foreigners' from
across the border. Well, I guess maybe he has.
They behave nice, he likes to show 'em off to visitors, and there's no use denyin' they've had more
of his candy than the others. They are the small-

est group of Natives, but because they're nighest
to the States, perhaps, they've bulked bigger in
our Uncle Samuel's eye than all the rest of these
folks put together. *They've* made the *first* port,
fine, thanks to the start old Father Duncan gave
'em.   But right now what I'd like is, if they'd
just forget the praise they've had and set sail for
an even snugger harbor.

"How?   Other Natives on this coast have got
their problems, ma'am, as Indians always have, I
guess, wherever they must mix with white folks—
who don't always treat 'em white, more shame to
us.   Because they've had such a good send-off, let
Tsimpseans put in with the other Natives, *I* say,
and help the whole crew on, to be good citizens,
not hold themselves apart as better.   That's what
they've all got to come to, if they're to stick it
out—with all the white folks moving in these
days, planning to make a white folks' country
here.

"I know a whole bunch of Southeast Alaska
Natives, bright as whips, smart chaps, well educated, like William Paul the Native lawyer up
to Ketchikan.   But that's a case of one man here
and there, branching out and taking up the white
man's ways—going farther on his own than Metlakatlans who've all held fast together.   Because
the whole crew here have got their quarters rigged

so shipshape, that sort of makes a deep impression, like. And because they are so solid, they *seem* the best of all.

"They're independent as fat hogs on ice, I tell you; and, as a lot, these Metlakatlans look as happy as fat clams! Whenever I hear people say, 'There are no good Indians,' I always wonder what they know of Metlakatla, where for once *some* Indian folks had half a chance, for a clean square deal of things."

III

Indian Sign Posts on the Northern Trail

> And they painted on the grave-posts
> Of the graves yet unforgotten,
> Each his own ancestral totem,
> Each the symbol of his household.
> LONGFELLOW.

METLAKATLA lies right under the plan-
tar cushion of the hoof of Diomedes' horse,
where Alaska first begins to rear aloft into the
North. To reach Father Duncan's village you
have traveled many hundred miles north from
Seattle, through the British Columbia portion of
one of our world's three great Inside Passages—
where ocean liners may steam smoothly along as
on a river, threading a narrow sea way that is
sheltered from the swell of open ocean by over-
lapping groups of many thousand islands.

From the moment one starts a journey Alaska-
ward, there is a glistening succession of Coast
Range snow-peaked mountains on the right, dip-
ping straight down to sea; while on the left the
countless islands in unnumbered hundreds stretch
on and on and out into the North, deeply spruce

blanketed, hauntingly lovely. Innumerable falls
thread down and water-streak these mountain
slopes while, as we near the North, ice rivers that
are glaciers hang in cupped valley-clefts or pour
down from the sky to break in bergs and float
away to sea. Here there are scores of glaciers
whose sea-detached fragments may be seen afloat:
in Norway only one like this—at Jökel fiord.

"The Thunderer," as the Indians call the
Hutli, sends out its floes for fisherman at Petersburg to gather—true glacier trove, to hook and
rope and break and pack their fish-catch in, so
they can haul it fresh to Ketchikan and Rupert.
The sea yields quintals here of silver fish, but it
yields ice as well on which your halibut is kept
sea-cool until it safely reaches you. At Taku
Inlet is a dual sight I doubt that one can see in
many other places. To the left, a dead glacier,
gray, earth covered and retreating, draws up behind the wide and terminal moraine between its
edge and sea. But on the right a glacier that
lives and moves, sharp cliffed in jagged abrupt
ice, breaks off incessantly in pushing toward the
sea, with thundering roar and crack, to drop its
ice tons for the busy fishing boats to gather if
they will. John Muir, that great naturalist,
drifted through this deep channel with his Indian
canoe, back in the seventies of last century; and

one gigantic glacier bears his name to-day, in memory of that great adventure.

These are the waters where the Thlingits and the Haidas have cast their nets and drawn their seines, time immemorial; and here to-day the powerful fish traps of the canneries run out a thousand feet to sea and snare home-turning salmon. Along these shores, light green of birch tree alternates with deep green spruce and giant green-black hemlock. You enter stilly fiords which seem to have no outlet, till the mountain wall suddenly slips apart to let you by, and closes up behind you. Here, silent sounds are milky jade in color, tinged by glacier-fed rivers. Glaciers thunder down to echoing far bays and ice-blue coves where tiny fishing villages cling fast to hill and shore. Snow-white peaks hang their bright tips high above the clouds, sheer mountain slopes are cut by down-flung fish streams, wide grassy valleys stretch back to those passes which lead to ancient gold camps—old trails, flower grown and spire tipped with a thick-set tapestry of spruce.

This is the roadway to America's Last Frontier—but you may see it from a steamer chair! There are few pioneer hardships, now, in traveling through Alaska's Inside Passage, but a winding stair of summer beauty leading securely

BEAR CUBS, "LITTLE AND FUBSY," AND FULL OF CURIOSITY.

A BABY MOOSE IS LIKE A CALF—ALL LEGS.

SOMETIMES THE ENTRANCE TO A HAIDA HOUSE
WAS THROUGH THE BOTTOM OF A TOTEM POLE.

OLD INDIAN SIGN POSTS ON THE NORTHERN

north. In '98, when gold seekers rushed helter-
skelter north of 49° upon that great new Forty-
nine stampede, this inland waterway was little
known, all but untried except by a few early
traders and adventurers. The argonauts of that
day crept to northward, to the Yukon camp of
Klondike, through then uncharted waters and in
old leaky boats that reeked of fish or seal oil.
The argonauts called that reek, looking back,
" the smell of the Yukon! " But up from 49°
to 54° 40', and on beyond to Skagway up at 59°,
is now a truly regal road, *El Camino Real.*
Modern twin-screw vessels, lighthouses, sea
marks, steam, and new hulls of steel, have made
true highway of the High North trail.

There are strange sign posts along this
northern waterway—sign posts that point us to
a primitive race and time and seem to carry us
far back and very far afield from the life of every-
day America. This Inside Passage to Alaska is
thickly set with grotesque totem poles, from
Alert Bay north to the land of Chilkats who,
while great carvers too, did not erect house poles
as did their southern neighbors.

Real totem poles are carved and painted tree
trunks, set up before an Indian house as a family
crest or name-plate, telling what people live
within, whence they came, who their kin may be;

or, used in ancient burial grounds as we set tomb-
stones, to tell the story of who lies there; or, in
some public place, a "story master totem,"
memento to some great event the people cherish
in their tribal memory—Trafalgar, Peace Monument, or Statue of Liberty. The idea underlying
totem seems to be as old as human history. Pre-
dynastic people of old Egypt were totemists, the
most ancient Hebrew story shows a trace of it, as
does the clan relationship of very early Romans.
The oldest Indian mounds in America appear to
be totemistic. Indeed, the notion is world-wide
in primitive people and our Saxon fathers held
to it while they yet lived in beech and oak-dark
European forests.

But what is "totem"? It goes back to
thoughts which every one, in childhood, held and
honestly believed: that animals are friendly, think
and talk as we do, have secret nature-knowledge
grown folks have forgotten, and can help us by
that friendly understanding, if only we keep close
our kin with them. "Alice in Wonderland" is
a perfected totem tale, while many of Grimm's
fables, most of early Greek myth, and the speech
of Baalam's ass, are rich and flavorsome with sin-
cere totemistic logic.

Totem poles aren't idols, as many people
falsely think. All up and down these dotted sea-

islands between the coast line here and the Pacific
(and, in some places, back behind the coast a short
distance into the interior) the Haidas, Thlingits,
and their kindred (and occasionally the Tsimpseans) erected totems to show *the Spirit favor-
able to their clan*. The clan itself was determined by blood relationship on the *mother's* side,
and the family totem will be crowned with the
symbol of the mother's phratry. South Sea
Islanders have poles not at all unlike these British
Columbia and Alaskan totems, and it may well
be that the first totem pole floated ashore here,
carried across the Pacific by the swirl of Japan
Current, borne along the coast of Asia and cast
up finally upon the shore at Tongass.

The old Indians believed that everything had
spirits, for the dawn-man is easily convinced (we
too, as children, were so convinced) that there's a
spirit like our own in all created things—eagle
and wolf, star shape and whispering wind. The
man who could best hear these spirits speak and
could best understand their voice, was by that
much above his fellows, a founder of new clans,
interpreter of mysteries. If a man could throw
himself into a trance, then—like the prophetess
of Delphi—he was communing with the spirits
who know much more of human destiny than ordinary mortals. Often fasting made possible the

seeing of visions, dreaming of dreams, giving the soul access to the spirit world; and perhaps this is why periodic fasting is a rite followed by the primitive " medicine " man or shaman, who was the " healer, sorcerer, seer, priest and educator." They said, to fast took a man's spirit away from his body and the things of himself and unstopped his ears to the talk of that other and secret universe. Thus he evoked, consulted, overcame the spirit world.

When the early Indian came out of his trance and told his story of spirit contact, it would often be of some mysterious animal—or some familiar animal—which spoke of magic, gave him mantic power. This animal he drew and painted upon all his possessions. He carved this animal before his house door, to remind himself and others that he had talked with spirits, now had super knowledge, and to suggest for all time the vision he had once experienced. As we have griffin, unicorn and salamander—all creatures " spawned in the fertile fancy of man "—rampant upon our national or family coats-of-arms, so too the Thlingit and the Haida carved mysterious beasts and man-like things, half bird, on massive trunks of trees; and these are totem poles—reminders of family ties and past events, of which one may be proud and wisely ponder.

At old Kasaan on Prince of Wales Island, once
Haida Indian stronghold, we find them; for
Haidas are the expert carvers of the Coast.
"Tongass" or Ketchikan, the early home of
Thlingits, is rich in totems. Chief Johnson's totem is peculiar here, for part of it is built into his
house. The low cabin is painted a bright pink.
Over the door and extending all across the front
of the house is an enormous painted whale with
widely gaping jaws, done in a rainbow spray of
colors. A totem pole surmounted by a bird that
looks like Jabberwock, stands straight and tall
as doorway sentinel. Chief Kyan of the Thlingit
people has a totem topped with a beaked bird,
wings folded, and below is a larger bird with
wings thrown wide, feet resting on a grotesque
bear—which tell to the initiated the bird descent
of his mother's people, and that he is also kin to
the great Bird and the Bear.

There is skill of a wild and positive kind in
these wonderful carvings. When we remember
the crude stone, bone or copper tools once used,
it is a marvel. And not only are these memorable pictures carven and cut but highly painted,
too, with singular Native colors, raw and vigor-
ous and very "modernistic" in their art, ex-
aggerated and grotesque. There's reason for all
this, good reason. The over-drawn catches our

eye, catches our mind. Dickens overdrew, and
his characters remain memorable. The carica-
turist and cartoonist over-draw, so that we catch
their point and satire in a flash, and read while
running! I know a famous sculptor's bust of
Beethoven in which the great composer's beetling
brow is violently accented, yet in that very massive violence the bronze proclaims the very soul
of Beethoven. And it is so that Haida wood cut-
ters conceived *their* art.

I'm often asked, " Are totems reverenced? "
Yes, just as we respect and honor our family
crest, a symbol of ancestral dignity and the pride
of race and place and cultural grace! But
totems are truly " family trees," not in any sense
graven images to be worshipped; and yet to bow
and worship them would be no sin against the
decalog, for they are unlike " any thing that is
in heaven above, or that is in the earth beneath,
or that is in the water under the earth."

There were the two great phratries, Raven and
Wolf,—or Eagle in some districts,—and under
each phratry were other animal emblems. William Paul's mother, for instance, has the right to
use the figure of a frog in all the carvings, paintings and embroidery which she owns. Marriage
was not permitted within the phratry, no matter
how distant one might be by blood; that is, no

Raven could marry a Raven, but marriage as close as first cousin on the *father's* side was permitted, since that would be between an Eagle and a Raven. That was the great law of the Thlingit people, and infractions of it were punished by death.

The old law is being broken, now, under the white man's law. I know that William Paul's younger brother married the daughter of old Chief Shake's nephew, she being also a Raven; but his mother collapsed when she heard of it and was sick in bed for a week! That is how strong *her* feeling is about this ancient marriage custom, even after a life-long absorption of the white man's thought and way. When she herself had been brought back from Victoria years ago, as a small baby, a great feast was given and a totem erected to expiate and explain away the " stain " upon the family honor caused by having a *Scotch* father—a clan not recognized as high in class, among these proud people!

The Eskimos, far to the north, also believe that two people of the same totem may not marry, and they too have a regular system of animal totem marks or family crests, with corresponding gentes or clan brotherhood. But because they have no great trees there from which to carve, they make no giant totem poles such as these in Southeastern

Alaska but only shape strange images like Billi-
kens, in ivory, and little charms—which may perhaps have a similar origin, way back in the dim
dawn of a gray break of time. Schwatka draws
pictures of grave-totems as he found them in the
eighties, among the upper- and middle-Yukon
Indians. But these are merely carven fish or
birds, perched on high poles like weather vanes,
fantastically painted, above the family burial
grounds. They are totems, and animal crests of
this type are indeed most widely spread; but they
are not true totem *poles*.

Father Duncan classified the Tsimpsean four
great clans of totems, as they existed in his day.
First are the Kishpootwadda, which have the fin-
back whale from the sea, the grizzly bear from
the land, the owl from the air, and the rainbow
from the sky for their symbols. The Canadda
have taken frog and raven, star-fish and bull-
head as crest marks. The Lacheboos deal mostly
with the wolf and heron, while the Lackshkeaks
are kin to eagle, beaver, dog-fish and halibut.
These are not tribal names, but family names.
As the surname " Smith " may mean that some
far-ago ancestor of yours was a blacksmith or a
silversmith or a locksmith, though to-day you
may be an Englishman or an American—so too
the Raven or the Eagle over a totem pole does

not mean "I am Thlingit" or "I am Haida,"
but: "My long-ago ancestor was once an air man,
kin to gods; and I'm his proud descendant."

While these family trees that make faces are
surely passing strange, yet in their roots they
are not utterly un-akin to us. I'm sure that you
know people of the wolf and raven phratry, even
in your home town. I do—a Dr. Wolf and a
Mrs. Rook. And the land is full of people named
for old totem families such as Crane and Fox,
Lyon and Fish. My own mother's people belonged to the Herron clan or phratry! Fine
ladies have a boar or griffin head engraved upon
their crests, which they will proudly display as
"totem" on the doors of costly limousine or
family plate or stationery. Horsa and Ethelwulf
are nothing more than good old Saxon totem
names that have been caught in history. And it
is not far fetched to say that Uncle Sam's own
children use the Eagle totem, British the Lion,
French the Cock, Russians the Bear, for these
are as truly clan symbols, significant of past
events and tribal histories.

An Indian from the southeast coast of Alaska
went for the first time to an Episcopal Church.
Telling of what he'd seen there, he said: "Shaman, dressed in a long big-medicine coat, read
magic from the top of eagle totem. He spoke

then to his Great Spirit while standing beneath
the totem of the sea-gull.   A beast with curly tail
and wings, a strange beast which I do not know,
was the totem cut in rocks over the door of this
council house."

Thus we ourselves are accused of totemism by
the child-mind of the Native, translating, as we
all do, the things we do *not* know in symbols of
the known; and we see here the Roman lectern
with its carven wing-spread eagle, the dove that
symbolizes to our minds the brooding and all-
hovering Spirit, as well as pictured Lion of St.
Mark—through the primitive eye, unmindful of
our rich palimpsest of Church history.

IV

The Red Man's Burden

Lo! How all things fade and perish!
From the memory of the old men
Pass away the great traditions,
The achievements of the warriors,
The adventures of the hunters . . .
On the grave-posts of our fathers
Are no signs, no figures painted . . .
From what old ancestral Totem,
Be it Eagle, Bear or Beaver
They descended, this we know not.
LONGFELLOW.

IN many an old New England attic corner you
will find a brass-nailed leather sea-trunk that
once belonged to some long gone sea-faring ancestor. Open that trunk and you will come on
mellow and parchment-crisp letters, dog-eared
log books, holding a record of long trading voy-
ages to the Seven Seas.

Ever since Captain Gray found the great river
on the northwest coast which he named Columbia
in loving memory of his vessel, " The Boston
Men " as Northwest Natives called them ranged
up that not too friendly coast in fur trade and in
barter. They sent back home, in rare passing

51

vessels spoken in sailors' gam, the tale of strange
folk whom they found here—a people of the same
Red Race which earliest comers found in the New
England forests, yet so artistic, so advanced in
many cultural ways that these observant sea men
had to marvel, and wrote their observations back
to stay-at-homes in a descripion of lost days that
are now almost utterly forgotten.

Long before Father Duncan gathered his
Tsimpsean pilgrims into Metlakatla, their kindred Haida and Thlingit possessed and held the
whole southeastern corner of Alaska, the land of
many islands. The alien Eskimos and their
Aleutian offshoots lay to the far north and northwest. A very different Indian, of Athapascan
Tinneh stock, occupied the great Interior of the
country. But the Haida and the Thlingit were
sea-dwellers, skilled in sea ways, and as such won
a grudging but very genuine respect from those
old captains out of Salem and Nantucket. For
these Haida and Thlingit Indians were very distinctive somebodies in America's earliest Who's
Who. Before they ever saw a "Boston Man"
or "Russ Man," they were doing several very
useful and artistic things superlatively well—
better than any other Indian people north of
Mexico.

Being a strong and warlike race, they set their

stamp on all who touched them. Chilkats, a
northern sub-tribe of the Thlingit up by Lynn
Canal, were not only tremendous fighters but
acted as middlemen in all the trade northeast and
northwest from this strategic point, into the body
of Alaska and Yukon Territory. Russians and
Hudson Bay men traded with the Chilkats here
for fifty years, without ever so much as seeing an
Interior Native; for the wily Chilkats had an
eye to profit and yearly took vast stores of furs
and copper from the less keen Athapascans, and
levied tribute, meeting the Tinneh at established
places many miles back from the sea. Chilkoot
and White Pass, later to become so famous in
the great gold stampede of '98, were but two of
their jealously guarded routes back into the
unknown North; and the very first white who
came across the Chilkoot, a red-headed Hudson
Bay man from Fort Selkirk, was promptly made
a slave by Chilkats the moment he set foot upon
their territory.

The masterful Thlingit held no exalted notions
about white superiority. They knew themselves
aristocrats, and their routes of trade and tariff
were kept forever sacred and high walled. Even
the conquering Russians of the brightest day of
Empire, who had enslaved the Aleut tribes and
made them work in constant and unwilling bond-

age—even Baránof, the Iron Governor, tremendous fighting organizer that he was—stood always in the shadow of fear from terror of the war cry of unconquered Thlingit, strong and skilled and unforgetting in their cunning. The Russians found their match in warfare here, the " Boston Men " their match in trade.

Who are these Thlingit and their allied people —red-skinned Americans of whom white-skinned Americans know so little and of whom they're willing to believe always the worst? To see them truly we should see them as those " Boston Men " saw, before white settlers came and before they suffered any change in those life ways which they themselves had skilfully worked out, from the resources of their chosen place.

They lived upon a coast that has a climate much like Scotland—in fact, Ketchikan and Metlakatla lie a shade further south than Glasgow, Edinburgh and Copenhagen—a coast rich in islands and in bays, the home of massy cedars. From Nature they had a fish diet to which they added berries and game and sea mammals. Their coats came from the shredded woven jacket bark of these same cedars, or from the white and woolly great coats of the mountain goat, which they wove into blankets; and from the black and pointed horns of mountain goats they carved their now so treasured potlatch spoons which, after years of seal-oil soaking, wear a rich jetty lustre undescribable.

A man's house indicates his living standards, and these men built such huge houses and of such heavy cedar logs, those early Yankee skippers marvelled. The tragedy is that so few of those great richly carven, richly painted dwellings remain for us to see and marvel at, to-day. From the giant hoary cedar forests, centuries old, they felled great trees by bruising off successive rounds of wood, used skids to roll them to the shore, floated and towed them down with dancing and with song of festival to the always-water-facing village site. Here they worked them out with adze and wedge made anciently of stone, and here they raised them at their feast times— immense, rectangular, roomy, communal houses sometimes forty by one hundred feet, with roofs like an inverted V. There was no Native wooden house of such a size and stoutness, so lavishly embellished, elsewhere in all America.

Vast patient labor went into getting out these huge trunks, in hewing posts and beams, forming the planks which made the ends and sides, and in erecting these massive structures. They painted the façade with mystic figures; the huge, heraldic, carven totem posts that stood beside it, fifty feet high and three feet at the base, were dignified and structurally beautiful. The end posts at the front were always richly carved with totem figures, done by special artists who were handsomely paid; and often the whole house front would be elaborately painted in a symbolical design. Any one could see that these substantial structures were the homes of enterprising people, master builders, utilizing to the full all the resources at their hand, showing ability to plan as well as execute. No wonder that Vancouver and other pioneer northwest explorers were loud in praise of these fortified townsites, striking and forceful and upstanding as the strong people who conceived them.

The house posts were set up at those great feasts, which early traders commonly called " potlatch." When completed, there was a smoke hole left in the roof, directly over that center where fire would be laid. Bare ground was left around the fire pit, about this a floor was laid, and a platform built all the way round the house inside, curtained and screened off into cubicles where the different related families, servants and slaves who occupied the house could sleep. At one end, at the middle of the back wall in the houses of the very wealthy, would be a carven " house pole " directly behind the fire, and here was the seat of honor. Here also was the stage, used for religious festivals and their dramatic presentations of myth and legend. Concealed openings formed by painted wall screens admitted actors who impersonated gods and heroes and wore elaborate carved and painted, richly decorated and intricately designed masks, symbolizing the Raven who became a man, or the Eagle or the Crane who could also take manshape. Regular clowns or "fun makers" gave songs and dances to the beat of wooden drums, realistic and magical sleight-of-hand performances. For these Indians' power of imitation and theatric invention was superb, highly apt in song and oratory.

Of all the early misunderstandings about the Indian, none was more ungrounded than that he had a crude language. The Native tongues were built up on different principles of grammar from European languages, were of so many dialects and sounded so unlike the European speech, that early comers (who were not usually skilful linguists, anyway) got the false notion that the Indians' speech was nothing but a gibberish, had a small number of words, and was really hardly human speech at all—much less an orderly and highly developed way of talk. The early comers thought the Indians used so many signs because they lacked words. Often they used signs because they found the whites so stupid!

Nor did the early comers always appreciate the sly and subtle humor of the Natives. Like all peoples living by or in deep forests, the Indian could be taciturn. And at his great ceremonies, when the first whites most often saw him, he acted dignified and solemn because that was the fitting way to act on such occasions. So should we act, in court or in a church; and I've no doubt a Thlingit who first saw us whites at a sitting of the Supreme Court, or watched an audience at St. John's Cathedral, would think *us* pretty solemn people, too! But he had a keen sense of humor tucked in his funny bone, up under the soft folds of his enwrapping Chilkat ceremonial blanket, and was no stranger to jest, to laughter, or to punning. The trouble was, the white man didn't know the language well enough to catch the point—and like the best of funsters, your Thlingit always kept a straight face when he joked.

The finest flower of fun is irony and he was master here, in his own house. We call a very fat boy " skinny " or a very tall boy " shorty," and Natives used this form of nickname, too. One of the famous Dakota chiefs was known —and is still told of in our histories—as " Young-

man-afraid-of-his-horses," and we who hear it
think he must have been a coward. But the name
really meant "Young-man-whose-*horses-even-*
are-feared," which tells a very different story!
Then there was the Kiowa name of "Stinking-
saddle-blanket"—as translated by some early
plainsman who was to prove a better rifle shot
than linguist! For the name was far from being
an opprobrious epithet, but told of daring and of
the tireless energy of a great fighter. Really it
meant what we mean when we say, a man died
with his boots on. For it was a compound picture word, to tell that this chief was so constantly
upon the war path that he never even stopped
to take the blanket off his pony's back, between
raids! Rough traders and early trappers never
caught the little hidden meanings here, the half
and quarter notes that play and sing, inside the
words.

Just so, there was a mighty Haida leader
whose name was translated by the Boston men,
"Unable-to-buy." You'd think that must refer
to a poverty-stricken soul, but really he was quite
the richest of all his people. The name was taken
by him, as names often were, after a great feast
when much trading had been done among the
visitors and guests. But this chief had a copper
plate, so large and fine and beautifully worked

that no one of the hundreds at the feast could afford to buy it, much as they'd like to. The name could better have been put into English: " He-who-owns-something-money-cannot-buy."

Inside these great wood houses were mural decorations and carved posts, beams, doors, and screens, all richly painted. For these Natives were not only master builders, but master artists. Their women were master weavers, too, and had uncanny skill in basketry. A score of household things were made of basket work—utensils, matting, and wall hangings—as well as clothing, cradles, wattling fence and weir. Gathering spruce roots, shredding, splitting, gauging, trimming, braiding, weaving, were women's work and they did it well. Cooking baskets were made of spruce roots, were water-tight when water-filled, and a hot stone immersed in them made " boilo." Mats for bedding, packing, seats and box cushions were made of pounded cedar bark, and the Haidas made a fanciful basketry hat of coolie shape, in beautifully checkered patterns and colors. One old Haida town was called " Village-where-hats-are-common." But the most widely traveled of the Boston men marveled most at the ceremonial Chilkat blankets, for they could see that there was nothing like them in rare beauty, among any Native peoples north of Aztec Land. Yet the Chilkat women wove them on the simplest form of loom, without a shuttle, heddle, batten or any other device, and with only a sketched pattern on a board to guide their unaided fingers.

The wild Rocky Mountain goat is a bearded stocky-shouldered cousin of the antelope family and, as found in the high hills back of this south-eastern Alaska coast, wears a rough pure-white coat, with horns, nostrils, lips and hooves pure black—a very striking-looking creature. In preparation for great ceremonies, the Chilkat women mixed a warp of mountain goat wool with shredded cedar bast, and hung this over an eight-foot horizontal pole set up on two forked sticks a few feet from the ground. All the details of the great, mythic, highly formal design were painstakingly woven in by a sort of Gobelin tapestry technique, so that even pictured life-forms took on a geometric character as the gorgeous blankets grew in shape. The woman sat before this crude loom and wrought her intricate pattern with deft fingers only, as does the basket weaver, with two or more weft threads. This colored pattern was outlined in black, and done in yellow made from moss, with delicate touches here and there of a soft bluish green, made from copper and seaweed boiled together. The de-

sign covered the entire surface of the irregular
shape, about six feet by three within the strongly
accented border line; and all the lower edge was
heavily fringed from unused warp. Far more
elaborate, subtly colored, and fancifully conceived than even the best of Navajo or Zuni
blankets, these lovely ceremonial Chilkats are the
delight and the despair of collectors to-day, for
now they're far to seek and hard to find.

Their staple foods were drawn from the sea,
and fish were caught in skilful traps, were cured
or cooked. Rustic poles set upon stakes were
hung with rows of drying red-meat salmon; and
these, outlined against the dark hemlock background and bark shelter-tents of summer fishing
camps, drew words of picture comment even from
the old sea captains, as they watched some Haida
grandmother pile up her fire of spruce boughs
in the dusk of summer evenings, lifting her wise
old head to test the wind that smoke might drift
all night against the drying fat-fleshed fish.
Boiled seal flipper was a special dainty; salads
were made of sea-grass dressed in oil. Clams and
muscles were eaten raw as we do, or dried on
sticks or bark for winter use. Vancouver noted
a kind of tobacco growing, and potatoes—sowed,
however, like grain, rather than planted. Berries
and roots were gathered and prepared and stored

in cedar boxes. So, you can see the great house of the Thlingit was a place of work and play and much good wholesome busyness, for everybody.

Indian wood-work reached a true apex here, where wood was bent by means of hot water and fire, then made into beautifully shaped, inlaid, carved and painted potlatch spoons, ceremonial batons, pipes in which willow bark was smoked, or clubs for killing slaves or enemies, salmon and seal. Curly knots of trees were utilized for wooden dishes, becoming useful vessels with only little shaping but usually carved or etched or painted with totem animal figures. Small gauge tubes were made of the long pipe-like stems of kelp that drifted on the rocks as tides rush in. From these, too, Natives made the worms for their rude *hootchinoo* distilleries, or split and twisted them to make their fish lines, fathoms long. Hardwood saplings had a core, which could be pushed out with a cane to make their larger pipes or tubes. In fact, all elementary wood-working processes were known and used except tenon and mortise, and in their place these Southeastern Alaskans worked sockets for frame timbers, pegs of bone or wood. In Tongass villages, Secretary Seward measured cedar planks four and five feet wide that had been cut out with nothing but stone tools!

Chests of wood were exceptionally well made here, and are among the choicest art products sought to-day by our museums. These large chests were used in storing food or clothing, for cooking (with hot stones immersed in water), for ripening salmon eggs, for holding seal oil, for drums, for the interment of the dead. Small children had box cradles, often, for papa had the adze habit and cedar was plentiful!

But the Haidas were the Caribs of these North Seas, because of their uncanny skill in boat building; and among these archipelagos of the North Pacific, from the mouth of the Columbia to Mount Saint Elias, the dugout canoe reached its most complete and beautiful development. Bow and stern, both high-pointed and carved, were sharp at the water line, graceful, and utterly unlike the clumsy wooden trough of the Mississippi Valley or the miserable bull-boat of the East and South. Cut from giant cedars and sometimes nearly a hundred feet long, Natives passed in the old days from one island to another in these great sea-going canoes. Each tribe had its own shape of boat as well as special pattern of bow or stern, ornamented with its own crest symbol—though they were usually painted black outside like a Venetian gondola, thwarts and bows being of brilliant red. No words can catch the flare and grace of line in these high double-peaked prows.

Haidas were the master craftsmen and hollowed their immense canoes by charring, and then removing the charred wood with a cutting tool. They sold their boats to other coast tribes, trading them for oolakan oil, copper, furs, baskets or dentalium. These canoes were valued according to their length in fathoms, and were to the Haidas what horses were to the Plains Indians. Living in a temperate moist climate, along this archipelago of land-locked waters, cut off from the Interior by high snow ranges, they traded far and wide in barter of copper nuggets and Chilkat blankets from the north, the spiky sharp black horns of mountain goats, teeth of the southern shark—rangers of the inland seas.

These people had unusually fine black slate for carving, as well as other stone for pecking, grinding, sawing. But the close-grained black slate was soft and easily carved when freshly quarried, yet grew harder with time and took an excellent polish; so on their plaques and dishes, Haidas from Queen Charlotte engraved designs that are true gems of art. One Haida carving in black slate of the Bear Mother " is not surpassed," collectors tell me, " in spirit or expression by any known work north of Mexico."

Without a metal-working furnace or use of artificial alloy, the Haida and the Thlingit were yet most skilful metal workers. They had a hammer and a cold chisel, etching tools for silver work, and made most handsome silver bracelets engraved with quaint and beautiful, highly conventional animal figures. Copper, which was plentiful, was used for ornaments, knives, arrow tips—was beaten into shape, the free ore merely broken, worked and hammered cold, as though the ores were stone. There was no smith's forge here, no potter's wheel, but a great deal of ingenuity and patience, time and muscle, knack of finger and observing eye, as well as artist's brain. The reign of stone began to totter when those first red copper nuggets were discovered, of pleasing color, taking high polish, useful, ornamental.

Dead races are unfortunately known to us only by their tools, their ruins, and their carven marks; but early Russian, British and Boston traders on this coast found a people very much alive—far too alive to suit their fancy!—and so have left a priceless record of the social life these people lived, their ways and manners and, to us, sometimes strange customs. Also, one of Alaska's women whose friendship I most value, (for she is one of its most able-minded) is the wife of that William Paul who is such a forceful personality among

to-day's Native peoples of this coast. To her
and him I am indebted for many intimate tales
of this proud and, in their own way, truly aristocratic race of people.

For caste reached its topmost pitch among
American aborigines here along this northwest
strip of coast; and distinctions of caste were here
most strongly marked and most religiously ob-
served. The low-caste groups were poor rela-
tions, people without any get-up-and-go, and
destitute people—not slaves. Sometimes there
were whole villages of low-caste people, much
looked down upon by the other villages. The
" elders " of the village held the rather loose reins
of government, and courage in war, wisdom in
council, power to speak well or to paint and carve
with skill, as well as any real or supposed psychic
gifts, could raise a man above his fellows; but
while this might sometimes react to benefit de-
scendants, chiefship was not inherited though one
must always be high caste to be in line for office.

The Thlingit were divided socially like the
Haida into the Yehl (Raven) and the Wolf or
Eagle phratry, each of which subdivides into
clans. Yehl was the hero-god of Thlingits, the
demi-god who by miraculous re-birth, " brought
back the sun " to chosen mortals. For like the
mystic Raven of both the Tinneh and the Es-

kimos, the Raven here was also a Promethean
fire-bringer, crafty and sly like Loki. Yehl in
his bird-shape stole the water, too, just as Odin
in his eagle-shape stole Suttung's mead in Bragi's
telling of the Younger Edda. Yehl is a " first
father," a great culture hero like our classic
Hercules.

Caste, too, was marked by manners and there
were certain things a high-caste person never did,
such as leaning backward or lolling in company.
When I was a child, my Philadelphia grandmother made me sit with both feet on the floor,
well forward on my chair, and never cross a leg
(for " Ladies do not do that "); and just so the
Haida thought it better form to sit alert and at
attention when in company. To be too frequently
a guest was also " low-caste " manners.

In many places and at many times in our
world's history, a very high-caste system has been
based on slavery; and slavery was very much in
vogue amongst these people. They made far-
distant journeys down the coast to get their
slaves, and counted private wealth in slaves,
just as did we white Americans of another
generation. Here was the highest stronghold of
slavery amongst American aborigines, and the
origin of their caste system. Because of this they
lived in settled villages, where slaves and the de-

scendants of slaves did all the heavy manual
work. There was a regular traffic in slaves and
slaves were legal tender, though in Interior
Alaska slavery does not seem to have been known;
but on this Coast, slaves were the most valuable
property a man could own. Captives were not
killed in war, but enslaved. Jewett (white
armorer on a wrecked vessel, himself for years
enslaved here) states in his 1815 narrative, that
" one chief had in his house nearly fifty male and
female slaves." Sir George Simpson of the Hudson Bay Company estimated that in his day fully
one-third of the Thlingit population were slaves,
the price of an adult being about $500 in Hudson
Bay blankets, of a child $150. Slavery in general
had virtually ceased, however, by 1890 and the
last case of which the Pauls know anything, that
of " Princess Tom," came to light about 1898.

Slaves were well fed and well treated, as was
natural with such valuable property. In most
ways they lived the same life as their masters,
whom they accompanied on hunting and fishing
trips, paddling the great war canoes which they
had helped to make, hewing wood, drawing water,
aiding in house building. Slave women and slave
children did all the housework drudgery, so that
the free women of these northern tribes were the
aristocrats and social élite of aboriginal women.

But slaves could own no property, and their masters held the power of life and death. Also, it was the custom to bury slaves in the deep holes dug for the posts of great houses, when such were raised, or slaves were sometimes killed during great mortuary feasts. At other times slaves were given away, or freed—a gesture to show that a chief was so wealthy he could easily spare some. Slaves held no civic or social status in the tribe, and any one marrying a slave automatically became outcast.

A woman's rank descended to her children and the children of the household belonged to the mother, not the father, always and by ancient right; for women here were actually citizens and did not have to agitate for " woman's rights! " Thlingit boys and girls played, as do all children, with toys and games, very like our own. In the summers, the whole village left their homes and went to their scattered hunting and fishing grounds, and here the children of the households had wonderful wild times in the woods. At the age of eight or nine, the boys were put under the care of their mother's brother, whose legal heirs they were, and who now began the so-called hardening process. The idea was that parents would be too lenient, and our own Middle English ancestors had a quite similar theory of education, you will remember, and sent their young boys as pages to be trained in others' homes. The Thlingit child was not punished, yet was very well behaved without punishment, controlled entirely by commands given in a low voice. Because it was believed that boys and girls became accomplished men and women by watching and by doing, pride and shame were the only whips these children knew, and their education by flattery or disparagement was the business of the entire clan, not merely their own parents.

" In the winter time, the days were occupied by the boys in gathering wood, a day's supply at a time," Frances Paul tells me. " When the early dark came on, the fire was built up high and the family gathered round to hear stories told. This was the real school of the Thlingit. These stories were the history of the race, mostly legend. But modesty, morality and a sense of right and justice were as natural to my husband's people as to us whites. Each story had a moral lesson, so well known that one need only to name the hero for the hearer to know what lesson was meant to be conveyed. They were taught not to be greedy, not to steal, not to ill treat animals—not even to ridicule an animal—to be grateful, to be strong-hearted—even the women: all the moral virtues that the white man knows. Each town had its professional singer, almost like a troubadour, who composed special songs for occasions and kept alive the old legends. And peace, not war, was the norm of the clan's life."

Then came the Russians, Hudson Bay factors, and the " Boston men," and with the coming of the whites these people passed at once into the Iron Age. They have adopted many white customs—most where longest and most constantly in contact with us, as in this section of Alaska; for summer tourists began to haunt this lovely islanded coast even before Lieutenant Allen, the first white man so to do, looked out from high divide into our long mysterious and unknown interior valley of the Tánana.

What do the Coast Indians think of our strange and different ways? From the *Verstovian,* official publication of the Sheldon Jackson School at Sitka, I have copied this word of an Indian girl speaking to her own people:

I have believed for a long while that the Indian race is now at the greatest crisis in all its history. If we can prove our fitness to live, we shall survive as a race. If we can not, then we shall be condemned to a slow death and nothing except a tradition of our past shall be left to the world. *You know the old life has gone.* And you know already, whether we wish it or not, a new life has come to take its place. And you and I must either go for-

ward on that new life or we must go backward.
We can not stand still. We have a greater task
ahead of us than any warrior kinsman of ours who
ever lived! It is an easy thing, under the impulse
of excitement and encouragement of war, to go out
and die on the field of battle to save your people by
this one act of bravery—compared to the strenuous
job of living day after day to the level of the highest that is in you. And that is the kind of living
you and I are called on to do. Because we are a
small group, in the midst of an alien civilization,
the focus of all eyes is centered upon us. Every
success we make, every failure we make, is conspicuous. Because we are such a small group, no Indian
boy or girl has a right to be a failure, for by fail-
ing we not only pull ourselves down, but we pull
down our whole race. Everywhere people are looking to us, watching to see how we are discharging
these responsibilities of ours. . . .

If our task is harder than our forefathers', we
also have greater advantages for facing it. Our
ancestors had only the traditions of their own tribe
to help them look into the future. You and I not
only have the whole Indian race at our command
but we have all the civilizations of all the world to
teach us. Any Indian boy or girl who wants it
bad enough may have all the rich treasures of education. Ought not our future history be greater
than any past record of the race? Would you not
prefer to live in this age and this generation with
its rare privileges and responsibilities? Your race
needs the best that is in you. And it needs you
more than it has ever needed you in the past or
may ever need you again.

Who knows but that thou art come into the
kingdom, for such a time as this?

V

GOLD!

Something hidden. Go and find it. Go and look
    behind the Ranges—
Something lost behind the Ranges. Lost and
    waiting for you. Go.

KIPLING.

WHEN Uncle Sam bought Alaska he
bought " a pig in a poke." He had no
notion what was really in that poke. Surely, he
did not think of it as a rearing young horse, nor
yet as a canny and strong, slowly-developing bear
cub. He looked on it, frankly, as a nuisance;
and I'm afraid some few who haven't learned the
truth, still think so.

This vast territory of then really unknown di-
mensions was bought from Russia back in '67 just
after the devastating War between the States,
when one whole section of the U. S. A. was still
laid waste by civil war, when the new transconti-
nental railroads were just beginning to link the
Far West with the rest of U. S. A., when gold
was at a post-war premium and our government

could least afford to spend a cent on anything not absolutely necessary. Alaska was not bought because we needed new territory to develop—for we already had what seemed enough for all time yet to come, in our nearer Northwest. It was not bought because we had any notion of the land's real value, for we hadn't. It was bought solely because Tsar Alexander wanted very much to sell just then and—because we very much owed him a favor—it was a courtesy on our part to take what he offered, especially at such a bargain price.

The older history books say that we "paid $7,200,000, gold," for Alaska. The actual price paid for the land, as we now know, was only $1,400,000, while the remaining $5,800,000 was *payment to Russia for her friendly naval demonstration* in San Francisco and New York harbors, at that time during the Civil War when things looked darkest for the Northern cause. Then, only an inner group of statesmen in Washington knew the truth about this, but now that "it can be told" we realize that Alaska only cost us about a third of a cent per acre, and that it has given back, to date, a jolly fat billion and a half dollars! That looks to-day rather like a good bargain; but in '67 Uncle Sam resented having to take the Bear Cub off Russia's hands. He wasn't

the least bit interested in Alaska, and for thirty
years thereafter he never even looked at it, but
let the wild thing rustle for itself. He was far
too busy with problems of reconstruction close
at home and with problems of the newly growing
West, to care about the cub of Russia now tied
by a legal string at his back door.

And then, one day in 1897, in the midst of hard
times in the States, an electric word flashed round
the world like wild fire. Gold, in unbelievably
rich quantities—placer gold, to be got for the
mere digging—had been discovered in the North,
very near—perhaps in—the District of Alaska,
for Alaska wasn't even a Territory then and was
looked on as a mere extension of wild-west Indian
land. But one July day in '97 a small group of
tattered men landed in San Francisco and stag-
gered up Market Street carrying moose-hide
pokes of pure gold worth three quarters of a million dollars, and within the same week another
little boat from the North put in at Seattle, then
a rather straggling sawmill town, bringing a hundred lucky miners and a million dollars of sub-
arctic treasure dust, confirming news of the great
gold strike in the Far North.

It was not long before the eyes of all the world
turned to the Yukon, and the ears of all the world
became familiar with a magic word—Klondike.

Within a few weeks, one of the greatest gold stampedes in history was on, and men of all races and all classes, men unfit and men unprepared, soft men from cities who knew nothing of the North at all, as well as seasoned prospectors from California, Colorado and Nevada—all swarmed aboard whatever boats they found and rushed off in a frenzied, gold-crazed madness into the mystery and the solitude of the North, from which a largish number never returned. For of those milling eager thousands who struck northward, that early fall of '97 and early spring of '98, only a few were wise, only a few were fit or equal to the spell-ful Yukon's tests, or strong enough to meet her stiff exactions. Rich placer gold was there, as rich as any strike of modern times; but of the thousands who went venturing so madly, only a few ever touched finger to it. Those who " drew blanks in the Klondike "—disheartened, cheated, broken, some by the rigors of the trail but more by their own weakness or by the cruelty and tricks of thieving gambling fellows who fattened on unfortunates—returned to say and so to justify their failure: " The land is harsh, austere, and awful, unfit for human habitation."

Some, though they did not " make good " in the North, told such tall tales of their adventures that we believed them super-men, the land a land for heroes only. Others, defeated, blamed the land and not their own lack of preparedness or skill, or common sense, or luck. These, too, told tall tales of the Yukon and, to excuse their own defeat, created legends that still live, such as the story that all north of 54° 40′ is land of a lost hope. Those few who made great fortunes there were even more disloyal to the land which gave them its top cream of richness, forgot the bounty and the source of bounty, and spent their latter days in luxury, elsewhere, without a single grateful thought or gesture backward, of leal or thanks. I do not know of a single lucky striker of those days who ever thought to endow a hospital in the North, bestow a fund for indigent miners, or build a needed road or trail or bridge. The ethic of that day was, rather, "grab and run." These ingrates, too, helped to build up a legend that the North is but The Land that God Forgot. It is not God who has forgot the North, but the ingratitude of men—lost weaklings of that great Gold Rush, who turned their backs upon their own defeat and blamed the Yukon for their own ineptitude.

But there were some who stayed, and they were winnowed seed of a New North. It is for them that Service wrote that song beloved of all who love the North.

" But the others, the men of my mettle, the men
  who would 'stablish my fame
Unto its ultimate issue, winning me honor, not
  shame;
Searching my uttermost valleys, fighting each
  step as they go,
Shooting the wrath of my rapids, scaling my
  ramparts of snow;
Ripping the guts of my mountains, looting the
  beds of my creeks,
Them will I take to my bosom, and speak as a
  mother speaks. . . .
Wild and wide are my borders, stern as death
  is my sway,
And I wait for the men who will win me—and *I
will not be won in a day;*
And I will not be won by weaklings, subtle, suave
  and mild,
But by men with the hearts of vikings, and the
  simple faith of a child;
Desperate, strong and resistless, unthrottled by
  fear or defeat,
Them will I gild with my treasure, *them* will I
  glut with my meat."

Whenever two or three gather together to-day
in Alaska, the talk will always drift to those
" early days " of '97 and '98, when pathos and
hilarious excitement, danger and fun, despair and
hope trod heel and toe, dogging one's steps upon
the weary trail. No one knew how to go, so all
the first ways were experiments, and all were
hard enough. Some took the yet imperfect maps

of the High North and—learning that the Klondike was a little river tributary to the upper Yukon, somewhere near Alaska's border—took boat
to St. Michael at the Yukon's mouth (a long
rough water way) and slowly worked the length
up-stream of that great river which bisects
Alaska. Some landed at the head of Prince William Sound or at Haines on Portage Cove upon
the southern coast and worked inland across the
ranges through elusive passes, got lost and finally
drifted into Eagle on the Yukon, after unex-
ampled hardships, for there was then no broken
way. Some started from the mouth of Stikine
River and worked up and behind the range from
Wrangell, following roughly parallel to the
coast the old and tough "Telegraph Trail" that
ran by Teslin and the Pelly River northward to
Yukon—"a pile of ifs and buts to *that* game."

And some—the most spectacular group—had
their goods dropped upon the beach at Skagway
or Dyea and took the trail up and over White
Pass or the dreadful Chilkoot—a way the very
Indians feared and where many an undisciplined
white trailer dropped in his tracks before he
reached the golden goal. Some packed with
horses, some with dogs or mules, and at least one
woman drove a team of goats! Some hired the
native Chilkat packers, at tremendous sums, to

Photograph by Cann.

A TÁNANA INDIAN BOY, WHO MAKES FINE AR-
ROWS AND HAS A BEADED QUIVER.

CHIEF HEALY OF THE UPPER TÁNANA WEARS
A WAMPUM COLLAR.

Photograph by Lomen Brothers.

"PLENTY FAT BAY-BEE IN HIM PARKA HOOD."

Photograph by Lomen Brothers, Nome.

TWO LITTLE MAIDS FROM NOME ARE WE.

carry outfits and a grub-stake up those towering
passes, over and down to strike the headwaters of
the Yukon—where they would rip out rough
small boats, shoot the wild rapids, ride the whirl-
pool, and *perhaps* reach Dawson. Most merely
packed upon their own bent shoulders all that
they took, back-tracking for re-portage, again
and yet again, until it all was over. Few knew
what " plunder " was the best to take, how best
to take it, or what route to take it by. 'Twas all
an untaught, wild, tremendous venture, an
equally tremendous gamble.

Don Adler tells you: " Travel? Chilkoot
Pass? Yeah, she was a tough one. Doctors, law-
yers, scholars, and working stiffs like myself,
climbing, sweating, cursing; and as they kept
climbing their packs grew heavier and they'd
start throwing stuff away. It got so, that if a
fellow only knew it, he could start at the bottom
of The Pass empty handed, and by picking up
things here and there, by the time he reached the
top he could have outfitted himself.

" Roadhouses? I remember one owned by a
little Frenchman—the place was about 14 by 16.
I got in a bit late. There were about fifteen men
in there then. No room to lay down, you just
propped yourself up against the wall. And each
man had his dog with him. Dogs were mighty

precious then and you didn't dare let them out
of your sight. And there they were, all jammed
in that little place—dogs that howled, socks that
creaked and threatened to break at any minute;
and the only cure for halitosis in those days was
liquor. I was pretty skookum in those days, but
half an hour in that hole was all I could stand."

Holes? There was one man who " grinded
on a snag in the upper river, bulged a hole in my
boat, and just by sheer luck I got to shore with
all my kit and boodle, plugged that hole up with
a side of fat bacon that was handy, snibbed a
plank cross it, and went on. She held fast, fine,
but that was a hard winter and my dogs smelled
out that bacon, ate it, and next spring, first time
I took the boat out, she sank under me and pretty
nigh drownd-ed me! "—Well, they were here, the
gold was there. They simply hiked out, one way
or another, only guessing all that lay between,
" in the corridors of silence, in the vestibule of
night." The marvel is, so many actually made
it!

" Placer " gold is loose, worn, powdered gold
washed down from hills where it was once " in
place "—that is, in veins within the solid earth of
Tellus Mater and now brought down, after long
geologic travel æons, into old creek beds, beaches,
marshes, shores, and combined there with loose

sands or gravels. If near the surface, placer gold is easily found, often by some mere chance and, because then it's also easiest to mine, placer gold offers always the most alluring enticement to any poor man. The individual prospector, with only his crude rocker, can take out a day's pay in virgin gold as soon as he has earned it, without asking any boss for pay cheque or punching any time clock. It's a product that, once found, requires no other capital than patience, muscle, and a slight grubstake to work,—a sack of flour, a slab of bacon, miner's pick and pan,—and once uncovered, is of immediate value directly upon being taken from the ground, without delay or loss or need of marketing.

These gold strikes, such as that of '49 in California, '97 in the Klondike, or later Nome and Fairbanks, are not exclusive modern things by any means. Ancient Egyptian records reveal that seventeen hundred years B. C. there was a gold rush to the auriferous land of Nubia or Nub (meaning " gold," some say) between the Nile and the Red Sea, with hungry gold-wild prospectors stampeding then, as now, from Caucasus, India, Asia; and for a century placers there were worked and many millions taken out. One of the most famous of all old Greek myths tells of a gold rush in the classic hero days—the Argo-

nauts, sailors on Jason's gold-seeking ship, the
Argo, after the Golden Fleece—so that to-day
the very word "argosy" has come to mean a
vessel carrying rich cargo.

Do you think of the Golden Fleece as merely
an order of the very highest rank, hung on a
golden chain about the necks of Austrian and
Spanish monarchs? Really, it was the symbol of
a gold rush, a placer-miner's token from that day
when Greek prospectors adventured far afield
into the distant Euxine or Black Sea country,
centuries before Christ. These miners had a
practice still being used in some remote places.
Instead of riffles in their sluice boxes, to catch
the heavy gold dust in its flow, the people of
Colchis used a rough ram's fleece to catch the fines
as they washed down the river, and hence The
Golden Fleece! But even to this day, the golden
fleece of placer gold is almost always guarded by
a sleepless dragon in the grove of Ares, and, in
the days of '98 as in those other days, the crew
would be of strange and motley blend: Orpheus,
Castor and Pollux, the two winged sons of
Boreas, Meleager, Theseus, Hercules, manning
the fifty oars of *Argo,* called "The Swift."

So every race and nationality of the world, with
all those strange mercurial types that have time
immemorial gone adventuring, found their way

to Klondike when that golden word was put upon
the wires. Billy Hudson who, with his wife,
brought the first piano into Dawson, freighting
it over Chilkoot Pass; Jack London and Robert
Service, two "winged sons of Boreas;" Sid
Grauman, later to be famed in Hollywood; Klondike Kate, the prettiest dance-hall girl of Dawson City, who "staked," men say, a handsome
young Greek immigrant named Pantages, a
suave waiter and muscular "bouncer" in one of
Dawson's many saloons; "Coolgardie Smith,"
soldier of fortune, who won and lost a dozen
rainbow-pots of gold, from far away Australia
to the Yukon, and who was first to shoot the
Whitehorse Rapids in a scow; "Good Egg"
Harvey, who "got a permanent squint in his off
eye, from candling petalumas for the old Alaska
Commercial—over-the-ice eggs they were, and
petalumas was both scarce and high, and to be
opened with prayer—or the other thing!" More
than one "lady known as Lou," loved-soiled and
passé, listened—with what thoughts we can but
guess—to the sour violin scrapings and the noisy
glamour when, elbow on bar and foot on rail,

"A bunch of the boys were whooping it up in the
    Malamute Saloon;
The kid that handles the music-box was hitting a
    jag-time tune;

Back of the bar, in a solo game, sat Dangerous
    Dan McGrew,
And watching his luck was his light-of-love, the
    lady that's known as Lou."

"Gamle Ole," Norseman at home by any
northern tarn or tor; Russians, "born in the
snow and living in the sun;" Kobuk Ned, Slisco
and many another dreamy South Slav; red-
blooded dissenters and social heretics a-plenty,
seeking their far horizons and, maybe, their
escape from clinging pasts; wild Celts, drawn
by the taunting other-worldliness so characteristic of the Yukon—so strangely seductive
to the mocking Irish mind; Cockneys, born
somewhere within sound of Bow Bells, wearing their birthmark branded on their speech;
good Scots, strong and sane and naturally philosophic, in this new land edging a little further from effects which do not matter and a little
nearer to their cause, which does; some crying
after old gods, some crying after new; foolish
and feeble, Hi-carders and Hi-jackers, "going
where It was and tying into It, from Soda to
Hoc"; some "childish, factious, ignorant, timer-
ous and ambitious persons," as Gorges wrote in
1607 at Sagadahoc; "fears of the brave and
follies of the wise," misfits and failures, the ad-
venturous and the contentious, all seeking refuge

in the wilderness, and change, or isolation or a fresh start or an even break—children and drunken men and fools, protected only by the uncovenanted mercy of Providence—and a few wise men and strong men, who knew exactly what they were about and went about it with but few waste motions.

On the dreaded White Pass, the summer following the great Klondike stampede two thousand horses lay dead and bleaching, grim reminders of that brief period when a spasm of gold-madness seemed to possess the world. Mushroom towns sprang up along these trails, " a violent eruption of camps," as one sourdough tells it, " like the pimples on a sot's face—impurities of a life drunk with glittering projects." The progress of any pilgrim there was beset with problems and Apolyons, " to test his mettle before he ever saw the metal," as one punning missionary put it. Wrangell and Skagway and Dyea were over-run by Soapy Smith's gang— an outlaw and notorious gambler who was called " The King of Terror " and ruined hundreds, by stealth or open murder. Another says of Dawson: " Everything wide open, and the sky the limit. That is, if you didn't overstep the law. Liquor, gambling and wild women were all okeyed, but if you stole another fellow's dog or his grub or his poke, then look out. The Mounties got after you and it was just too bad for you.

"However, hardly anybody stole in those days. You could go along the trail, enter a man's cabin, and if you were hungry you were perfectly welcome to help yourself to some beans or anything else. The chances are you'd run across a poke of gold on the shelf, or even right out on the table, but you never touched it!"

At Dawson and its near-by gold creeks, the North West Mounted Police saw to it that offenders did not exactly languish as Her Majesty's guests while serving sentence, for they put prisoners to work, even at forty and fifty degrees below zero, sawing wood and at non-union hours! Prices of food, those days, freighted so far and at such a cost of time and effort, were desperately high and most of the new-won gold went down men's throats, one way or other. "Sugar was higher than a cat's back," one sourdough tells me, "and two fried eggs—the frozen-out kind—cost three dollars at any eatin' house. An' gamble? Say, those gamblin' chaps was that persuasive, I'll tell you, that by the great bullet-eyed catfish, they could talk the crook out of the hind leg of a spavined horse!"

Out of this heterogeneous mass of shared experience grew a strange comradeship, a curious loyalty to one another and to the North, the Arctic fellowship of the true Sourdough, with yeast-pot, bacon slab and rifle for his grubstake. Leaving Canadian Dawson where the Klondike Creeks were over-located, the flood of men spilled on into our American Alaska just across the way, discovered gold here, too—at Nome, Valdez, Fairbanks, the Iditarod, amongst " the wiry willows of the weary Kuskokwim," and a score of other camps—and here remained to seed a new empire in the North. Out of the rich soil of a shared experience, too, has grown a vocabulary peculiarly Alaskan: *cache* from the French, and " mush " for trail travel, from the French trapper's cry of *" marchons "* to his dogs; *tillicum* for pal, *skookum* the Indian term of approbation, " moose " for large (as " he's a moose of a man ") ; " cleanup," and " pan " and " poke " from California mining terminology, and a score of other words from Russian, Spanish, French and Indian roots, but all so typically Alaskan, now. Strange minglings!

They came, again, to Nome in 1900 when " Gold! " was cried upon that distant Alaskan beach. One tells me how he went, up from the port of San Francisco in a sailing vessel, forty days at sea catering across the North Pacific, a

smother of foam upon her bow, trailing a long
white wake. He learned to handle canvas and
not to fear aloneness, lashed aloft there to the
royal yard, amongst the black night and the stars
—tending her sheets and braces on the sloping
deck when, wind upon her quarter, the boys clung
to the log reel as the line whizzed through the
hand of the Kanaka mate. Those were the days
when an old clipper bow under living canvas
could yet shame the straight-stemmed and me-
chanic steamer, whose wake to-day overlies that
of the sailing ship as auto highways overlie the
Indian trails. So, to the ice-blown Bering Sea,
and the Camp of the Spoilers.

Nome? Vessels which took men to that strike
were so overcrowded, they tell to-day the tale of
one man, third day out, going to the captain to
ask for a place to sleep.

" Where have you slept, to now? "

" On a sick man," was the answer. " But he is
getting better and doesn't seem to want me to! "

And coming back, with plunder and with
treasure, what tragedies! One " lucky Swede "
(all Scandinavians are called " Swedes " in the
North!) had made a small fortune and, being
cautious, and hearing that all those who carried
heavy gold dust pokes Outside were apt to be
robbed either upon the boat or after reaching Se-

attle, had his "stake" turned into thousand-dollar bills and sewed within his shirt. His "bunkie" on the long homeward trip, a jolly Irishman, complained because his pal wore that same grimy shirt, day in and night out, never changing. He kidded and plagued the Swede to change, but he would not—of course, and for good reason. But one night they got him heavily drunk, stripped off the offending shirt, threw it overboard, and put a clean shirt on him as he slept.

That awakening was supposed to be a joke—but the jest failed. The half-awake unfortunate gave one horror-struck look at the new shirt, and in half-incoherent babble of wild words demanded the old. His roommate only laughed.

"You'll never see *that* dirty shirt again, old timer, and good riddance. 'Twas filthy—and I threw it overboard. You've a clean one to your back now, like a white man, and you should thank me."

The other looked at him with dull awakening comprehension, groped his way to the rail and —while his plaguers looked and laughed and then went cold with consternation—threw himself into desolate Bering Sea and was never seen after. The Irishman was rich, and would gladly have "made good." But it was too late.

Yet sometimes these cruel jokes turned otherwise, as Fate flicked unexpected cards. Two men
in Dawson rolled and frisked a drunken miner
for a $500 poke of dust, leaving in his pockets a
quit-claim to a " fraction,"—a worthless mine
they had,—thinking, if he should later make com-
plaint to the authoritics, they'd swear he bought
the quit-claim for the poke. That " worthless "
claim proved to be worth millions, panning $10,-
000 to the foot! Truly, " the Northern Lights
have seen strange sights."

There were long trails when all the food gave
out, and " we high-graded the dog salmon and
chewed boot leather, that year when we made the
Kaltag portage." And there is Jennie Cleve-
land's saga of North-coming in the summer of
'97, with the first shipment of drygoods to reach
the Dawson camp, over that White Pass which
had broken the spirit of so many men. Skagway
swarmed with adventurers seeking the elusive
metal, but tales of lurking danger held no terrors
for her and, dogs being at a premium, she
strapped a harness to her own neck and shoulders
and tramped the long, snow-burdened trail of
heart-break across the wind-wracked spirit-rack-
ing Pass—to arrive at Dawson in the fall, later
conduct a roadhouse at Bonanza Creek, join the
Nome stampede, haul the first sawmill outfit into

Mayo, try her hand at mining in the Fortymile, and fetch the first team of horses into the new-found Fairbanks camp in 1904. She pioneered again at Dome Creek and the Hot Springs and, in her busy life which touched so many tangents of the North, grubstaked more out-of-luck pros-pectors than any one I know.

And here is another sourdough record of those days—in " I Remember When " of spotted story:

Cold weather? Why boy, you ain't seen nothing yet. I remember . . .

Back in the winter of '99, my partner and I were walking into Dawson from Bonanza creek. Fifty per cent. of the thermometers hit bedrock and went to smash, and those that could withstand Old Man Win-ter's heavy hand registered between 73 and 74 below.

And that's cold, boy. You can't hold a conversa-tion—if you say anything your words freeze, and the fellow you're talking to has to take the frozen words into a warm room and thaw them out before he knows what you're talking about.

Anyway, we headed for Dawson to celebrate Christ-mas Eve, and we stopped at every saloon along the way; and there was one of them to be found at about every other claim. By the time we reached Dawson we didn't know whether it was 73 below or 173!

The smallpox epidemic? Yeah, I remember that. Every one in Grand Forks was quarantined. I remem-ber a lady asking me to help her get out so she could get to Dawson to fill a heavy date. The Mounties were watching us all pretty close, but we sneaked out, came down the Klondike and later I deposited the lassie at her destination. Went into the dance hall to play up against the fiddle (dance), and a few minutes later a heavy hand landed on my shoulder and a Mountie asked me how the blankety blankety blank I ever got out of the Forks. I didn't know what to say, so he threw me in the jug to give me time to think up a good story. A few minutes later the lady was thrown in to keep me company. The Mounties certainly had a close checkup on everybody everywheres! But the lady didn't mind because she had cleaned her Date by that time!!!

Marriages? Remember the time Old Joe wanted to get married? He brought his lady-fair up to the judge's house, where his Honor and I were in heavy consultation over the merits of the various brands of hootch . . .

" I want to get hitched," says Joe. " Sure," says the judge, and wabbles over to his book stand and reaches for a Bible, picks up a heavy book, places the man and woman in front of his desk, looks down at the book and then says: " You take this lassie for . . . for . . . everything? " Then turning to the lassie, said, " You . . . you . . . do the same with this fellow? " The answers being affirmative, he then went on with: " Well, I do hereby hitch you together so that four horses can't pull you apart. That'll cost you five ounces." And then, after the couple had left, we looked over the big book and discovered that the old judge had married them with a MONTGOMERY & WARD catalogue!

" Yeah . . . them was the days."

VI

The River that Rises in Mystery

The trails of the world be countless, and most of the
    trails be tried:
You tread on the heels of the many, till you come
    where the ways divide . . .

And somehow you're sick of the highway, with its
    noise and its easy needs,
And you seek the risk of the by-way, and you reck not
    where it leads . . .

And sometimes it leads to the Northland, and the
    scurvy softens your bones,
And your flesh dents in like putty, and you spit out
    your teeth like stones . . .

And sometimes it leads to an Arctic trail, and the
    snows where your torn feet freeze,
And you whittle away the useless clay, and crawl on
    your hands and knees. . . .

ROBERT SERVICE.

TO-DAY there is a railroad, wonderfully con-
structed, that climbs White Pass from
Skagway and reaches down upon the eastern side
of the divide, past the dread canyons and the
rapids, until at Whitehorse you connect with safe
and comfortable river boats. The journey on to

Dawson, now, is quite another matter than in those hectic days after George Carmack, with Indian Kate his wife, discovered gold " while fishing under the Old Birch Tree, up Klondike way." There's change, to-day, upon the Yukon, since that time when " cheechako spuds " were a rare luxury, moccasins were being worn to dances, and " dust " was currency across any counter.

You cross over into British territory not twenty miles from Skagway-on-the-sea. A tiny pond lies near-by in a pocket of the hills, a pond filled with dirty snow-water drained down from higher summits. Yet this mere cup of water is of strangely curious significance, for it is one of those very small things which can be strong enough to turn the course of history.

From one side drains a tiny stream which tumbles swiftly down to sea level in an unhampered, careless, useless manner, like ten thousand other insignificant cascades. Perhaps one stone, a little lip of mud, were first enough to turn a similar trickle spilling from the other side, in quite a different direction, to quite a different history. Deflected, this right-hand stream turned, twisted, bent and doubled, finding a way through miles and miles of barren hills, cutting whole provinces, watering an empire. Adding allies as it goes,

augmenting, developing, enlarging, it travels
more than two thousand miles before it reaches to
the sea at last, but in that journey has become
meanwhiles one of the greatest river courses of
the earth, shaping incalculably the destinies of
men; for this cup of slushy ice-water is, with the
Nisutlin, the embryo of the Yukon! Alaska's
rivers clearly teach Alaska's children to be far
wanderers. The Natives say of the Yukon: " It
comes down from the Mountains of Mystery, and
vanishes into the Valley of Nowhere."

I've lived beside this mighty Yukon highway
summer and winter, trying to read its secret.
There it lies, always at one's door, calling, calling.
I've followed it from that spilled cup on the
divide down to the place where river empties into
sea—and back again. The Great River of the
North has come to mean to me a symbol of life's
self, shaped by events which cut out unexpected
channels, down which the course must run. Rising in mystery up within dark highlands, The
River flows broader and more resistless, unhast-
ing and unresting, down to the equal mystery of
the frozen sea. Along its course are nearly all
varieties of scenery known to man. Sometimes
you seem to be in the Scotch Highlands, sometimes in Norway and again in Tyrol, or upon
Saint Lawrence, Hudson at West Point, or again

the Rhine: vast timbered stretches, a thousand
mossy hills, scores of great putty-colored cliffs
and massive granite walls, picturesque fish camps,
salmon wheels innumerable lazily turning with
the current, mining towns both big and little
though most are merely now deserted tiny camps,
Indian and Eskimo villages as well as the brave,
small settlements of white colonists, Russian,
Catholic and Protestant missions. Always the
River's self is gaining with its shared experience,
in dignity and volume and in breath. There are
shallows with their treacherous bars where sound-
ings are every moment necessary; and there are
rapids, so narrow one may almost touch the rocky
walls as one sweeps swiftly through. The River
goes its patient and resistless course, changing
daily the details of its banks but never altering
the great, sure, predestined outline of its way.
All life seems held within the Spell of the Yukon.

The River rolls its patient way to sea, a
twisted and meandering way of countless bends
that, all stretched out, would reach from Washington across to San Francisco. Drifting down,
in a slow river boat, you see a band of caribou
upon the near-by hills. Those on the " Texas
deck " catch sight of a black bear, fishing at the
water's edge, and so the captain toots the " game
whistle " to call attention and bring the other pas-

sengers " top side," and Ursus, greatly startled,
scampers for the tall brush.   The slow deep pant
of the great engine breathes through a night that
is not night—for at Fort Yukon you are north of
Arctic Circle and in late June you can see here
the sun at midnight reach down to the *north*
horizon, crawl along it for what seems like half
an hour, then rise again without having once
dropped below, blending to-day with to-morrow
in one perfect glow of rose-gold sky and molten
rose-gold river.

All along Alaska's southeast and south coast
the mountains rise literally from tidewater. There
are no coastal plains there drained by great rivers
but only relatively short streams interrupted by
falls and rapids, that empty swiftly into the sea
and offer no open door from that side or help in
entering and exploring the vast domain beyond.
But in the Interior the Yukon threads its way
through our mid-northern woods, treeless tundras
and sub-arctic plains from east to west, one riffle
after another, "like some great mighty thought
threading a dream."   Yet Americans in general
know less about the Yukon than they do about
the Congo! Like Siberia and like northern
Canada, which are Alaska's nearest neighbors,
this land behind the ranges is rich in rivers that
reach clear back into the heart of the country and

bring down furs from the hinterland. And twisty rivers they are, too. Joe Crosson, one of Alaska's famous air men, says, " From Iditarod to Holy Cross by air is only sixty miles, but by the River it is just four hundred! "

The greatest tributary of the Yukon from the south is the Tánana, which rises in the high near-coast mountains but flows west and north until it merges with the Yukon " about thirty miles below the Ramparts, and its rapid waters increase the current of the main river for a long distance." So Lieutenant Raymond wrote in '69 of this then unventured great river of the North. The Indians near the southern coast had massacred all Russians who attempted to cross over that way to the Interior, so people for a long time only guessed that this great river was really the Missouri to the Yukon's Mississippi.

The greatest all-Alaska tributary to flow into the Yukon from the cold side of the Arctic Circle is the Koyukuk, which comes down from the north and east with such a push it turns the Great River sharply south through three degrees of latitude. You open up the mouth of the Koyukuk at Nulato, and can travel more than 800 miles on it to the villages of Allakaket, Bettles and Coldfoot, the latter near to Caro on the Chandalar.

Emil Engstrom tells me of prospecting on the upper Koyukuk and on the Chandalar in 1907, in the days when one " pan " (which holds about a shovel and a half of dirt) contained $1800 worth of " pay." This was the richest pay dirt to the pan I've ever heard of in Alaska. Engstrom went into the supra-arctic with his brother, pulling their camp outfit themselves with a neck harness; for as he says, " We could not afford to feed a dog team after we got in, and few men have the heart to kill their dogs when they no longer have use for them. To keep awake and pull a sled when it is 73° below, takes a lot of will power! My feet had been badly frozen, and it was my third experience, so I looked at my toes almost every night for several weeks to see if they were turning black. Over 400 miles as it was to a doctor, I thought at times of amputating two of my toes with a red-hot cold chisel.

" That spring the flower of the original sourdough prospectors had gathered in the Koyukuk and Chandalar. They were the last of the true western frontiersmen and they dreaded the approaching civilization more than anything else. They were on their last retreat; one more move north and they would be on the border of the Arctic Ocean. Only the high Endicott Range, which we could see on clear days, separated us

from the sea." These were the experiences men
had, blazing these empty spaces—before the railroad and the airplane came to eat up space and
break down that long time-wall, which shuts us
from the rest of all the world in isolation and in
solitude.

The Kuskokwim is another great Alaska river,
second only to the Yukon in length. They run
parallel for many miles, almost touch at one
place, and both flow west into Bering Sea.
But the Kuskokwim is little known to white men,
even in Alaska. Here Russians built their forts
and set up trading posts in early days, as on the
lower Yukon, and the Alaska College at Fairbanks has recently been given one of the old Russian block-houses established here over a hundred
years ago, which will be re-set-up upon its cam-
pus. This was originally built by " Creole
Luke "—Ivan Lukeen, born in California of
Russian and Spanish parentage and educated in
the Russian school at Sitka—who was later murdered by the Indians. The fort had a little cannon in it, a stockade, seven large roughly-built
frame dwellings, and a long warehouse. There
was a chapel, too, built on the timbered mesa,
well above the river. This post marked the limit
of Eskimo trade up river and Indian trade down-
stream; so, like Nulato and the influx of the

Tánana, this little fort of Russia was in its day
a true outpost of empire, in that —

> " Land where the mountains are nameless,
>   And the rivers all run God knows where;
> There are lives that are erring and aimless,
>   And deaths that just hang by a hair.
> There are hardships that nobody reckons,
> There are valleys unpeopled and still.
> There's a land—Oh, it beckons and beckons!
> And I want to go back—and I will."

VII

Potlatch and Wampum

Thus the Birch Canoe was builded
In the valley, by the river,
In the bosom of the forest;
And the forest's life was in it,
All its mystery and its magic,
All the lightness of the birch tree . . .
All the larch's supple sinews;
And it floated on the river
Like a yellow leaf in Autumn,
Like a yellow water-lily.

LONGFELLOW.

WHO were the native owners of these inner lands, before the white man found them and took for himself these great and patiently meandering rivers, rising in mystery and flowing ever into the Unknown?

A very different Indian people live here than upon the Southeast Coast—different in language and in look, in habit of life and in degree of skill. No great cedar mansions rise along the Yukon, for there are no great cedars here behind the ranges but only smaller trees—birch and spruce and tamarak—brave trees that grow in soil that is forever frozen, just below the mat of moss which covers much of all the inner land. No deep tap-roots go down, to bear the burden of a giant tree, but only outspread mesh of roots, twined underneath the moss; and any burning over or high wind will topple trees in windrows. And no great log canoes are here but slim canoes of birch, framed on ribs of tempered birch. For the Tinneh of the Inner Lands are the northern-most cousins of that widespread Athapascan Indian family, noted travelers who covered all the Northwest of the inner continent in open shells of portable birch bark.

A hundred thousand miles of inland waters, bound by short easy portages, were their trans-continental highways; and in the bark of silver birch the Tinneh found an ever-present treasure. Of bark he made his cooking ware, his plates and platters; for where bark is so plentiful, he found no need to invent pottery. Boats and houses grew upon the flanks of trees, spruce roots be-came yarn, twine, or rope under his women's fingers. Wallets, baskets, cradles and cooking pots were all of stoutly-made, bound, stitched and folded water-tight birch bark. Dishes were of bark, vessels for storing fish-roe in underground frozen caches, as well as platters and trays for serving or for drying food, and many stout boxes.

And when the catch of caribou was good, and bear and red fox, wolf and rabbit made winter meat and warm fur winter clothes assured, their women found the time and fancy to embroider, either on moose-hide or on birch, the loveliest patterns done in porcupine quill—an old-time Native work now passing, but very, very lovely at its best.

One of my choicest Indian treasures is a round Tinneh birch-box, about three inches high and ten in diameter. The lid is very neatly fitted, and every inch of the whole outer surface, except the base, is covered with embroidery of porcupine quill. Upon a solid background of the natural-colored, pearl-gray, sable-tipped needles, in the very center of the cover is one beautifully pointed graceful leaf, done in short quills dyed a soft willow-green and worked in crewel design so skilfully, that the quill stitches form the natural ribbing of the leaf. It is the best piece of that once so common ancient quill-work I have seen, and while I own it and can show it, no one shall say to me that " Tinneh Indians have no eye for beauty " !

But art is flower of leisure, and the Tinneh lived in lands where Winter is months long, and bitter cold. Their ancient winter houses, to conserve the maximum heat, were half dug out in pits along the river terraces, set in the sloping hill—the door an underground passage by which one went *down* to the entrance tunnel, ten to twenty feet long, through which one crawled on hands and knees just as into an Eskimo igloo. The sloping roof of poles and bark, or sod, alone projected above ground; and in the very center was the smoke hole. The entrance of the Yukon houses always faced up-stream or east, the fire-pit lay beneath the smoke hole, and about the walls were shelves which served as bunks, the master's bunk always opposite the entrance. To-day the Yukon Tinneh have adopted white man's log or frame cabins, but you'll find the entrance still facing toward the east.

In each Tinneh village was a *koskónon,* the " big " or " meeting " house, large enough to hold the entire population and at least as many more guests. This place was like the lodge of eastern Indians, and here the winter dances and celebrations of all kinds were held, the feasts and shaman's magic parties. There was no slavery here, no caste, and Tinneh hadn't even any word for rich man before the Russian traders came and brought the name of *toyon* with them, from Kamchatka!

But don't think for one moment that these Tinneh were poor in words. Far from it, for they have a most pictureful language, rich in strong metaphor; and if figures of speech make poetry, then these crude Indians, who so dearly love strong metaphor, are surely your true poets. When they saw their first airplane, they came excitedly to Fairbanks from up-river and told us they had "heard motor-boat in sky" and seen "moose-ptarmigan." Moose being their largest animal and ptarmigan a white bird, surely "large-white-bird" is not an unpoetic name for airplane! They call a phonograph "canned white man," which is rather apt, I think. Bishop Rowe tells how he once selected some Indian dogs for a sled team and, when he had picked out those he fancied, he asked advice of the old Indian who was with him. One special dog impressed the Bishop as being very fine, and likely to make a good leader. But the old Tinneh shook his head.

"But why not?" the Bishop insisted, rather nettled.

"Too-long-time-dog," the Native said. A picture way of saying "old," wasn't it? I love their rooty metaphors. One Tinneh called his elder brother "the-one-who-is-aging-ahead-of-me," and a Tinneh man will not refer to his wife by name but will say "the-one-I-love," "the-one-who-gave-herself-to-me." A Tinneh of the upper

Tánana came one day to ask for lard or " fat,"
and was given a small pail. He said nothing,
but made no move to go. The trader asked, im-
patiently, " What's the matter with it? "

" Fat-too-young," the Indian said. What *he*
wanted was a grown-up pail!—It's like a guessing game, to catch the figure of this speech.

Tinneh words are really little roots of words,
that can be compounded in any shape or form,
" agglutinated " or stuck together to make a constantly new variety of meaning. They're usually
of one syllable, these roots, though the made-up
word may run to eight or ten syllables and express a very complex idea. But the noun and
verb roots of which they are built are simple
sounds such as *to* (father), *on* (mother), *ten'a*
(child), *keh* (birch), *tseba* (spruce), *ses* (black
bear), *yes* (wolf), *kun* (fire), *tu* (water), *kon*
(rain), *so* (sun). These I have from Father
Jetté, long a devoted Jesuit missionary amongst
the Tinneh of the Yukon Valley. The Tinneh
have a rolled "l" like the Welsh, that's very
common in their language, and it crops up so constantly when they try to speak English that their
speech is apt to sound like California Chinese!
" Maybe lain, maybe snlow," they say, if asked
about the weather.

When Dall came down the Yukon in 1866, he

found these people " almost in a state of nature,"
so he said, and without much or any material culture.   It is a climate where the winters drop to
40, 50, 60 below zero, where game will often mi-
grate for long seasons, too, and hunters have to
follow game.   The Indian is not generally nomadic, as we falsely think, but usually stays
rather closely within a certain bound or tract.
But these Athapascan Tinneh, because they knew
no agriculture before the whites came, because
of these vast wide stretches of great river courses
which they must follow for their food, as well as
the migratory nature of the caribou and other
game and fish they lived upon, of necessity
changed places frequently and couldn't know the
fixed, secure, rich village life of Thlingit or of
Haida.   And so, of all the American Indians,
they most nearly do approach a really nomadic
way of life.

The cruelty of northern winter has crept into
their tongue.   Their speech is full of terms of
cold and hunger as, speaking of a hard winter,
one will say: " We saw of cooking, nothing but
the fire! "   And many an Indian tale begins: " It
was in the fall, the ice running."   One of our
northern missionaries told me how he struggled
to make out some way he could translate to them
the beauty and the meaning of Isaiah's lovely

phrase, " the shadow of a great rock in a weary land." Yet the words were so packed full of metaphor telling what the warm East knew and loved, but what the sun-lost winter North could never know, he tried in vain to find the Tinneh words that would express the inner meaning. The blazing desert of hot sun, *they* would imagine Heaven (if they could imagine it at all), and a shadow could mean only chill and cold.

Then, traveling on a long, lone winter trail and coming at late dusk to one of those blest shelter-cabins which our government built, in early days, for the rescue and relief of tired and weary men, he had an inspiration. By his little Yukon stove of fire, over his meal of tea and rice and frozen fish, he wrote down in his notebook: " A hiding place from the wind, and a covert from the tempest; as rivers of water in a dry place, *as a shelter-cabin upon the black and lonely winter trail.*"

And when he turned this English into Tinneh and read it to his little band of Christian Natives, they nodded heads in eager understanding, and were comforted.

Kathleen Newton is a dear Fairbanks girl of English parents, now my neighbors, who lived her childhood upon the upper Tánana among the Tinneh there. She called to my attention how very light-skinned Tinneh babies were when

little.   These tots with big brown eyes and
straight black hair, are carried most times on their
mothers' backs, wrapped in a blanket that is held
in place by a strip of moose-hide or caribou, tied
under mother's arms.   These baby-bands are
sometimes heavily beaded, and I have a lovely
band like this, done in a pattern of native wild-
flowers.   The Tinneh children seem easily
amused and have fewer toys than Eskimo or
Thlingit youngsters—not that their parents love
them less, but because they have to work so hard
and move around so much to get a living, they
have less time for toy-making.   Tinneh parents
never seem to say " don't " or " no " to their children, but as there isn't really very much in these
simple households for a child to cry for, they
aren't at all the spoiled babies you might imagine.
One thing I've noticed is that they don't seem to
have as many " pretend " games as we do.   But
the boys have their toy arrows, and begin quite
early to go hunting with their fathers, learning
to endure real hardship with stiff-lipped uncom-
plaining.

" We never could understand some of the
Indian superstitions," Kathleen says.   " They
will so often say a certain thing must not be done,
but they don't like to talk to us about their reason
why.   Perhaps it is such old tradition that they

have forgotten why! For one thing, our Indians simply would not swim. There is hardly an Indian in our part of Alaska, except those taught by the missionaries, who can or will swim. One old Indian once told me that they don't swim because, if they do, a big fish will come and eat them! They seem to have a notion that there is some monster lurking in the water. It seems to me that people living by such beautiful summer lakes and swimming places as we have on the Tánana, are missing a great deal if they don't swim in them. But if a Native can't see the bottom of the water in the lake, he is afraid and suspicious of it, as he is of death and other mysterious things he cannot understand." But I myself think that the real fact back of this superstition is the silt-laden water of our great sluggish rivers, which drags down even the strongest swimmer. So many have been lost in these rivers that a tradition of the monster may well have grown up; and the Tinneh didn't make any distinction, as we whites do, between the heavy and silted river water and the clear and light lake water.

"Another unwritten code of the Indian," Kathleen says, "is that they must not destroy the carcass of any fur-bearing animal they have caught. On the roof of almost any old log cabin or cache you can see the skeletons of different animals, some many years old.   No matter how hungry the Indian is, he will not eat this meat or feed it to his dogs.   They think that if they do destroy these bones, the whole precious fur species will die out, whereas if they carefully preserve the bones, more animals will come.   And so the man who has the most skeletons on his roof— and not in his closet!—is the luckiest hunter.

" When an Indian kills a caribou or moose he never leaves the antlers on the ground but hangs them on a bush or in the branches of a near-by tree.   I don't know any reason for this, but when going through the woods, it is a common sight to see antlers white with age hanging on a tree."

I've heard a typical sourdough yarn about these hanging horns, told by an old prospector when he was asked by a gushing cheechako, " How do the caribou get their horns back every year, if they shed them in the fall? "

" Well, it's like this, ma'am," the old sourdough said.   " You see, the caribou don't generally have no use for horns, come winter, and there's precious little use of carryin' round that mort of heaviness upon your head, unless you need it. So, come autumn, they just hang 'em on some windfall, like you would your bonnet on a hat-rack, ma'am—until next spring, when they go back

and duck their heads into their own pair of horns
again, and are off!"

The creamy jest was, I believe the cheechako
really swallowed this tall tale! She never
twitched a smile.

Kathleen says that "Indian dogs are just as
cool and self-controlled as their masters are; but
these dogs—poor things—are nearly always
hungry, for an Indian will never under any cir-
cumstances kill a dog, though he thinks it all
right to let him starve to death! An Indian-
trained dog will never take any meat or fish from
about camp, unless it has been expressly given to
him; and I have seen dogs, pitifully gaunt and
thin, go wandering round a camp where fish was
drying easily within reach, some even on the
ground, and yet they won't so much as look at it.
But our Indians will often bury a favorite dog
with just as much ceremony as they use in the
funerals for their own kin."

A Tinneh Indian doesn't think it right to use
dog-skin for fur. He will give you two reasons,
one very practical and one wholly sentimental!
Unless very elaborately tanned, a dog-skin always retains a certain odor, offensive in damp
weather. And so the Tinneh say that people of
really refined nice tastes and delicate feelings,
don't use dog-skins for clothing. If, in the tell-

ing of a story, a man is described as " one-who-
wore-dog," then all the listeners will make throaty
noises of disgust and disapproving interjections
meaning " Shame," " Dirty fellow," " He-no-
good." But the sentimental reason is equally
strong. The dog is the only domestic animal the
Tinneh knows. His very word for " tame " is
leka, dog, and when the Tinneh first saw tame
caribou or reindeer he called them " caribou
dogs " or *ranoy-leka.* The dog is an intimate
member of his household and shares all the family life, as does the Arab's horse. The Tinneh
says: " Dlog-pup-sklin all-slame lil' clousin. No
wear dlog-parka, no wear parka my-dlead-
brother. All slame, parka-no-glood."

Like all Indians, the Tinneh dearly love beads
and use them profusely. In the old days, they
not only embroidered in quill work but, long before the Russians came and brought their blue
Bohemian-made trade beads, these Interior
Indians carried on flourishing barter with Chilkat and Copper River tribes and got from them,
for bales of fur, Pacific coast wampum or dentalium. This precious shell, which lends itself so
well to decoration, was traded inland so extensively that dentalium has been found as far east
as the Dakotas! Our Tánana Indians seem
more skilled in beadwork than any other Alaskan

tribe, and use bead trimming generously on their moose-hide coats. Porcupine quills could be colored in bud or root dyes, to yellow, green, blue, black or red and so used for trimming. But they were hard to work, while tooth-shell or dentalium was a white and hollow, glistening, natural tube, easily strung as a long bead. This shell is from one to three inches long, and can be worked into necklaces, bracelets, belts or scabbards. Coast Natives found it in sheltered harbors and inlets, buried in the sand in four or five fathoms of water; and they patiently prodded for it with long-handled broomlike brushes, along shore in their canoes. The women strung these shells on shreds of dried sinew, and a " forty-to-the-fathom " strand bought a male slave among the Thlingit, or two female slaves. " Wampum-peag " in the East meant merely " white shell," and this white shell of the Pacific also became currency, easy to carry and to wear as purse or bill-fold.

In the spring or " Time-of-the-hard-crust " the Tinneh go a-hunting, a few days' snow-shoe journey; and if there's meat, they will speak happily of these excursions as the time when " We were sitting in the shelter of the spruce trees, leaning our backs upon them." Later, while waiting for the River to break and the time

of running ice, the man draws sketches on the
sand for contour of his bark canoe, plants a row
of sticks along that line to form a hollow mold
in which the flexible strips of birch-bark are next
laid, about the bent ribs and frame. The woman
sews these strips together with small split roots
of spruce, puts on neat patches to cover holes and
cracks. She has been busy gathering pitch, and
now she caulks the seams with hot spruce-gum,
until everything is tight.

When summer comes, then old and young (including even " one-moon-baby," and all the little
Indian boys and girls, with shy big eyes like small
wild animals) go in these birch craft to their fishing camps, where the summer salmon catch is
made, and live there in their temporary bark or
skin tents, roasting fresh salmon before an open
fire on sticks, gathering berries. In the fall, they
follow moose and caribou as they move down
from the hills, and the first winter snow means
getting out fine-meshed toe-turned-up snow-
shoes, the snow staff, and the spear for opening
water-holes. It means the winter parka, too. Of
one woman who was not a good seamstress, I
heard a man say: " Once she made a parka for
me, but when I put my head in it, it was as stiff
as birch-bark cradle! " But usually they are
soft and pliable and all securely sinew-sewn.

When Tinneh folk die, their friends and kin make songs about them and sing these songs at the gathering feasts. One chant like this I've heard, sung by a brother for his sister, had the haunting refrain: " O the fine soft glossy parkas that she used to make! O the soft parkas!" The women made a coiled-work basket, too, and men carved wooden dishes, buckets, trays, and long-stemmed wooden ladles, painting them red and black. These potlatch spoons are often very handsome.

The winter feasts and ceremonies are many, the winter nights are long, and there is need of much good entertainment. The Tinneh love good stories and so story-telling is considered a great accomplishment. Curled up along the wall of the winter house, feet to the center, the last man to " roll in " puts out the little light. Then some one says, " Who has a story? " And some voice in the dark begins to speak. It makes no difference how often they have heard this story, it is always good and always believed! After the first sentence it is polite for some one to cry out, " *Anni!* "—Good, go ahead, that's fine! The story teller speaks slowly, in a low tone, as though he crooned a tale there in the dark, and peals of laughter, exclamations of pity, sympathy, disgust, puncture his telling. The story

begins invariably with, " In old times, it is said,"
as our best stories always start with " Once upon
a time "—for the race's childhood is the age of
its best tales. But the story always ends with:
" That is all. I have chewed off a part of the
winter! " or " A part of winter is become short."
For what are good tales, but a means to shorten
Winter?

A man would save for half his life-span, to give
away all of his wealth in one grand gesture which
ranks him ever after among the great men of his
people. Unlike our Carnegies and Rockefellers,
the Tinneh did not give what they could spare
but literally all that they had. Nor do they turn
away sorrowful, but face a new beginning at middle or old age, with courage and with faith. The
Tinneh families gave frequent feasts, generous
presents, and practiced an unbounded hospitality. Having so very little, they gave everything;
and when a guest would spend the night with
them, not only was he fed but his torn parka or
worn boots were carefully mended by the women-
folk, in the dim light of winter cabins.

Greed is a quality we are apt to consider
" primitive "; but in December, 1927, old chief
Thomas, gifted shaman, gathered three hundred
of his people for a ten-day feast, for which he
had been years preparing. He gave away about

DOGS THAT LOOK WOLFISH ARE VERY APT TO HAVE WOLFISH TRAITS.

Photograph by Cann.

HURLEY'S RACING TEAM OF THOROUGHBRED SIBERIANS—ALL SMILES.

A WOLF, CAUGHT AND USED FOR BREEDING
ALASKAN SLED-DOGS.

THEN I LEARNED TO DRIVE DOGS MYSELF.

$15,000 worth of goods, and after the potlatch the old man owned nothing but the house in which he lived, for he is one who still believes the Indian can be happy only in following the old way, and that the white man's way is not for him. Others, such as Arthur Wright, believe the potlatch a bad custom.

Potlatch itself is not a Tinneh word but from Chinook trade jargon. The local term is *whu-telth,* and when a feast of giving is to be, the word *whu-to-du-telth* goes far and wide. Then all come in on the appointed day and there is singing, eating, wrestling, dancing to a drum, much talk, and the " tea song "—after which, when the pot is emptied, it is slung along the floor with loud shouts. Dance shirts are put on, hats stuck with ribbons and feathers, while empty baking-powder tins with pebbles inside are used for castanets, held in the hand while dancing.

There is the happy dance, the sorry dance, and the dirge or mortuary chant. The happy dance is best, but after days of this strenuous life everybody is pretty well tired out and the giver-away is destitute and must take charity for the rest of the winter. For this reason many of the missions are trying now to abolish the custom and a few of the younger men realize its economic evils. But the older people cling to the older ways.

Deer meat or fish was boiled in the old days in birch baskets or wooden bowls. Fish, fowl, duck, muskrat, hunks of deer or bear-meat were roasted by the fire on sticks stuck on the ground. One ate from the pot, as did our Saxon kinsmen; and although knives and forks were lacking, so were they in the palaces of European kings, not many centuries ago! The only serious charge that I've heard brought against the Tinneh as a friend and neighbor is that "He's dirty!" Yet I myself have Tinneh friends whose houses are as modern and as clean as any in our town, whose food as well cooked and as nicely served. When we remember the few years that have slipped by since the first white man found this hidden inner valley of the North, behind the piled-up ranges; when we remember the noisome London of the early Norman kings set on its "right unclean marsh," or how Black Death and Sweating Sickness once stalked those offal-strewn streets: then we should be willing to pardon even the very worst of Indian villages. We ourselves are so short a time removed from habits of insanitation, we cannot carp or sneer at those who are not finical about "dirt," but should rather set a good "clean up" example. Not all white traders, here among the Tinneh, have been immaculate in person!

Besides, Indians and Eskimos alike practiced

the sweat-bath, an heroic form of bodily cleansing
that few of us hardy Nordics would care to follow! Each tribe had different methods, but few
practices were so nearly universal. Among the
Tinneh, a man made a sweat-hut for himself of
small willows with their thick ends stuck into the
ground, intertwined and fastened with strips of
bark to form a very small round tent. Over this
he placed a canvas or a moose-hide. In the old
days, hides were used. Just outside, rocks were
heated almost red hot in a fire and then placed
in the tent, sticks being used as tongs. The Indian would then go inside, taking a little water
in a bowl and a small bough, and close the opening to the tent. With the bough he sprinkled
water on the hissing hot rocks and made a quantity of steam—so much that on coming out he
looked like a broiled live lobster! Nevertheless
he would run down and plunge at once into the
ice-cold river. It seems to me that body pores
were well opened by *such* a process, and personal
" dirt " well sweated off!

I cannot call a people with such Spartan habits
" dirty." Like Father Duncan's Metlakatlans,
these people too are eager for any " good ways "
that we can teach or show; and Father Duncan
found the best way to his Natives' hearts was
soap, you will remember, and that's a way not

un-akin to godliness! Not all great races of the
past have made a fetish of cleanliness. The
Greeks did, and the Romans. I wonder, did the
glory that was Greece, the grandeur that was
Rome, come because they were such a bathing
people? Or did they wash, because they *were* so
cultured and so " civilized "? The mead-halls of
our Saxon forebears, when Grendel stalked those
northern moors, were not entirely dirt-free. And
what was the sanitary rating of the court of English Alfred?

Plenty of political " dirt " gets into histories,
nowadays, but mere physical dirt seems beneath
your true historian's dignity, even when it lies
unquestionably beneath his nose! Dirt doesn't
mix well with ink-pots. The science of public
health is a new product, of the second quarter
of the nineteenth century; but our Tinneh
stepped out only yesterday, from the very middle of the Stone Age.

VIII

Black Sun and White Night

The summer—no sweeter was ever;
  The sunshiny woods all athrill;
The grayling aleap in the river,
  The bighorn asleep on the hill.
The strong life that never knows harness;
  The wilds where the caribou call;
The freshness, the freedom, the farness—
  O God! How I'm stuck on it all.

Service.

THERE is no word quite big enough to give an adequate impression of Alaska's huge size.

It is one-fifth as large as all the U. S. A. It holds nearly six hundred thousand square miles, or as much as California, Oregon, Washington, all the New England States, New York, Pennsylvania, New Jersey, Maryland, Delaware and West Virginia—with Hawaii and Porto Rico thrown in to fill up some of the remaining chinks! Alaska stretches as far north and south as the distance from New Orleans to Duluth, as far east and west as the distance from Washington, D. C. to San Francisco. Its coastline is longer

than that of all the forty-eight states put together. The highest mountain in North America
is a part of its south wall, and just one of its
many glaciers on the coast is larger than all the
glaciers in Switzerland. Yet it is such a land of
paradox, most people have no true picture of it.
Indeed, the very thing most people think of first
in thinking of Alaska—the Klondike gold field—
isn't in Alaska at all but just across the border
in Canadian Yukon. Alaska has many fertile
gold fields of its own, however, and many of to-
day's Alaskans are sourdough Klondikers who, as
" Old Man " Cragie says, " shook the snow of
the land of the Maple Leaf from our moccasins
and staked a new claim under the folds of Old
Glory." For the North is really two countries,
under two flags: Alaska and Yukon Territory.

Alaska's delegate to the International Association of Navigation in 1926 represented " more
miles of navigable waters than any other delegate
present." Alaska has the largest bears in the
world—the famous Kodiak. Alaska has only
some twenty-thousand-odd white colonists to-
day, who are its soldiers of empire; but it is second only to populous California in gold produc-
tion, and it possesses one of the world's richest
copper mines as well as one of the best paying
lodes of gold. And coal is here, in plenty and in

the landing fields for planes. And these are white men's towns, composed of people very like myself—and very like in mind, I thought, to those who came across once on a time from England, to make a colony in our America.

I found that nearly every house here had its lovely summer garden of vegetables and flowers, its own electric-lighted henhouse and a hothouse built at its rear for tomatoes and cucumbers and early lettuce. I found that the summer day here was fully three months long, and that one never knew when night came, for the sunlight never ceased in all that period; and so the warmth kept piling up, and things grew in a lush and almost tropic way. I found that winters were indeed quite long, and that our inmost portion of Alaska was truly very cold, at times. But I also found that, when coldest in the Yukon Valley, the air was quietest, and in the "deep cold" (below minus 40°) the air hung breathless still. I've never seen real blizzards here, as I've known them in New York State or Colorado; but I have seen three people overcome by heat—in my own town of Fairbanks, on the day when President Harding was here! I've never seen one of those dancehalls, of which Service wrote so vividly, for they passed with the old wild days of '98. Even the most far northern towns, such as Dawson in Yu-

kon Territory, Fairbanks and Nome in our own
Alaska, now have their courthouses and incorpo-
rated civic governments, are law abiding, and
are settled by groups of men who see ahead long
years of decent wholesome living and whose master bias is not get-rich-quick but making " happy
fireside clime to weans and wife."

A far cry, you will say, from days of '98? But
that was something wild and passing. What's
seen to-day is the enduring mettle of our pastures, for it is based on gold and copper and other
precious lodes in place, on great wide seams of
coal, on valleys where the best of richly glutinous
northern wheats ripen and grow under the midnight suns, on tundras where a million reindeer
fatten for the market and other countless feral
caribou and moose and mountain sheep range
in the hills, on wooded streams where salmon
climb to spawn and all the finest fur-bearers of
the North pit their beast canniness against the
trapper's patient skill. This is the North, to-day.

When you think of Alaska, you have to think
in Brobdingnagian and not Lilliputian scale, if
you would think truly. This is not one empire
but many, and most people in the States don't
discriminate between the part of Alaska which
lies north of the Yukon within the Arctic Circle
—the land of Eskimos and polar bears; the Tem-

perate Zone middle province of Alaska, which is like the Middle West or New England; Southeastern and Southern Alaska, which have a climate very much like San Francisco or Seattle. William H. Seward, in his " Travels Around the World " wrote from " Berlin, Sept. 5.—We have seen of Germany enough to show that its climate is neither so genial, nor its soil so fertile, nor its resources of forests and mines so rich as those of southern Alaska." And our Judge Boyle of Juneau went out to Milwaukee last winter and couldn't stand the cold, after being used to the mild climate of Alaska's capital. So he spent the holidays in Pennsylvania, which seemed more homelike!

There really is Arctic life as well as Arctic climate to be found in Alaska, but they are just about as far removed from Ketchikan or Metlakatla as Labrador is from Florida—are in certain sections of Alaska only, and only in certain definite seasons of the year. So big the land— and yet apparently so easily mislaid and forgotten, by those " Outside! " Perhaps the Bear Cub has not growled enough, to remind our Uncle Sam of his growing-up existence here, tethered in Uncle Sam's north lot.

I lived three years in a radium mining camp, above that part of western Colorado called Para-

dox Valley. Here the river cut through high
mesas, ran paradoxically across a valley floor, not
down it, and cut again into the opposite hills to
join the strangely beautiful and wild Rio Colorado. All of Alaska is a Paradox Valley, it
seems to me, because all opposites are found here,
and much that's found is opposite to expectation!
Though lying so far north, much of the climate
is relatively very mild and warm, because all of
Alaska's great stretch of Pacific coast is washed
by warming Japan Current, which bends the
isothermal lines far northward and makes the
temperatures depend much more on distance
from the sea than distance from the equator.
And though it is a land containing many great
glaciers, these are paradoxically in its southern,
not in its Arctic section—because only on the
high mountains of the Coast is snow precipitation
heavy.

Though all the southern coast is moist, due to
the constant sweep of these sea currents, the Interior has often not enough snowfall for good
sledding and, in the part that's nearest the North
Pole where you'd expect it to be coldest and
snows deepest, there winter temperatures are
modified by sea-nearness, and sea winds often
sweep the thin snow from the land and leave it
winter bare! While in winter the Southeast Coast

has the climate of Seattle and San Francisco
(flowers in Skagway were growing in the church-
yard, on December second of the mild winter of
1929), the Interior has the climate of Bismark
or Butte, and the north coast has the climate of
northern Scandinavia or Russia. In summer, the
Southeastern Coast is more pleasantly cool than
Washington, D. C. because it is so intimately
sea-modified. The Interior gets so warm in summer that we complain about it, and the grain
crops ripen overnight—that " night " which isn't
night, but a white light; and on the northern
slope of the Arctic rim, the livid tundras keep
their not-so-long but all-continuous summer tryst
with life and warmth, by blooming in a flood of
blossoms.

And so, you see, the question of Alaska's
" cold " cannot be answered with a simple " yes "
or " no." As I once wrote in a " contemporary
ancestor " letter from the colony of Alaska:
" Alaska is, above all, a land of paradoxes, and
one is tempted to say that there is *no* statement
of physical fact that can be made about Alaska,
of which the exact opposite can not also be
posited, and with equal truth! To phrase this in
pure Alaskanese, you can play it straight or
copper the bet, and stand to win good money
either way. For instance, one may call the coun-

try wet, cold, mountainous, inhospitable, barren,
undeveloped, icy, dark, inhabited only by savages.
Every one of these statements is strictly accurate,
of certain places and at certain times. One may
also state with absolute certitude, however, that
Alaska is dry, warm, open, hospitable, well-
watered, well-developed, sunny, light, and inhabited by the venturesome pick of the Nordic stock.
These statements are equally true, of certain
places and at certain times! It all depends upon
which list you, temperamentally, incline to believe, or which one the limits of your Alaskan experience have tended to verify."

Some people still seem to think, like Adam
of Bremen back in the eleventh century, that
" All those regions which lie beyond, are filled
with insupportable ice and boundless gloom; "
whereas in reality many Alaskan summer vistas,
like those in Scandinavia, show a frame farm-
house resting in golden meadows that are rich in
peaceful sun-glow. As for Alaska's towns—
well, the Alaska College at my own home town
of Fairbanks, lying just beneath the Arctic Circle, offers a course in landscape gardening!
Stefansson the great explorer, born in Manitoba
of Icelandic ancestry, is very impatient with
those people who still think of the North as un-
livable. He says, " I will devote myself seriously

to the abolition of the ' polar ' regions. The aura
of mystery surrounding the North is a pall of
ignorance."

When I was a youngster, there was a poem in
the school reader which we all loved to recite—
Saxe's " Blind Men and the Elephant." Surely
you remember it—about the blind men who went
to *see* an elephant, and each brought back a different report because each had touched but *one
part* of the huge animal, and so each got a totally
different and false notion of what an elephant
was really like. Groping about, one touched the
dangling tail and so decided that elephants were
like ropes. Another bumped against a leg and
proclaimed to all the world that elephants were
like trees! Another felt of the beast's broad
flank and so insisted ever after that elephants
were merely walls; while the men who happened
blindly to touch an ear, or tusk, or trunk, got
other very different partial pictures—a fan, a
sword, a snake—and each insisted that *he* was
right, for he had actually touched an elephant
and knew!

Many tourists to Alaska remind me of the six
blind men of Hindustan. They touch Alaska but
touch one section only, or at one time of year
only. They don't see the whole body of the
country steadily or whole, but see one frame only

of a film that moves and changes always, in all its parts. They take away most curiously blind pictures. Because they had expected to find dog-sleds here, perpetual snow and many Eskimos—even in southern Alaska and even in summer—they bundle up in Eskimo parkas which they have rented, and with perspiration dripping from their faces they pose and have their pictures taken to send back home. So they perpetuate the silly false notion that *all* Alaska is the land of Eskimos, that the summers are not hot, and that the people ordinarily wear Eskimo parkas.

Parkas are as useless in southern Alaska as fur coats would be at Miami. Even in Fairbanks, where my home was for so long, people in general never wear parkas. I happened to have one which I bought from my Nome Eskimo friend—one she had made when at Herschel Island, well within the Arctic Circle. Mushers on winter in-land trails wear denim parkas, fur trimmed, as wind protection in medium cold weather. We don't travel in deep cold—colder than 40° below zero—unless forced to, and even then you can keep warm if you keep moving, or if you don't get wet in the overflow of glaciered streams.

For, strange to say (another of Alaska's para-doxes) the streams here overflow when weather is coldest. Very cold weather freezes ice in any shallow stream clear down to the creek bed. Water coming down from the hills has to go *some-where*, and so it rushes out *over* the ice, on top of it, making an overflow, and this water, and not mere cold, forms the most dangerous thing to be winter-feared in the North. More sourdoughs have died from frozen feet, caused by an overflow, than from any other accidental cause I know.

By yet another paradox it is the sun—the friendly sun, giver of life and father of heat—which is, with water, the source of many another grim tragedy of the North. You know what happens even in mild north temperate climes, when "the sun turns north" at and after the vernal equinox: how it lingers later, how dazzling bright it seems if there be any snow upon the ground. All this is doubly, trebly, and incredibly true, near and at the Arctic Circle; for here the sun does not inch up a little further each spring day, but *rushes* north. Each part of earth gets the same total amount of sunlight cast on it, year round; but because the Highest North has not had any sun at all in midwinter, and the Middle North but a few scant moments of sun at midwinter noons, with spring the sun appears to hurry back as though to make up for lost time! Summer Earth turns her north portion toward the sun (after it was turned away from sun all winter) and North gets now the full continuous glare of the great luminary. In spring, before there's heat enough to melt the snow, this glare of gold on white is truly blinding.

The wooden eye-shades of the Eskimo are best for this. In fact, the Eskimos have invented so many clever ways of meeting northern problems that, in general, the nearer we conform here to their ways, the less liable we are to meet with disaster. Then, too, old sourdoughs tell that a poultice of wet tea leaves on the eyes will cure snow-blindness, almost overnight; and every hunter carries tea in his kit. But spring snow-blindness has sent many a man, lost and in agony of splitting eye-pain, unable to see or shoot, to tend himself or dogs, to follow any trail—all those who had forgot or did not heed the inexorable Law of the Yukon, that bids one surely wear slit eye-protectors at Black Sun Time—

" Staggering blind through the storm-whirl, stumbling
        mad through the snow,
  Frozen stiff in the ice-pack, brittle and bent like a
        bow;
  Featureless, formless, forsaken, scented by wolves in
        their flight,
  Left for the wind to make music through ribs that are
        glittering white. . . .
  —One by one I weeded them out, for all that I sought
        was—Men."

IX

" Mush, You Huskies, Mush! "

'Twas a malemute first scaled the Chilkoot,
  At the time of the great Klondike charge;
'Twas a malemute first saw Lake Bennett,
  Left footprints across Lake LeBarge;
They hauled the first mail into Dawson,
  That Land of the Old Timer's Dream,
And when Wada first drove in from Fairbanks
  He was driving a malemute team.
  PAT O'CONNER, *Alaskan Sourdough.*

WE saw Alaska from the very first, I think, through a dog's eyes, for we took our Monte with us all the long way from Seattle when we first came in. But Monte was a thoroughbred Airedale and so a " pleasure dog," Alaskans would say, while your true dog of the North is a " work dog "—the huskies and the malemutes which made the early development of this country possible. They were to the winter trails what the slow chugging river steamboats were to the summer trails; and to-day, auto roads and railroads and airplanes are surely superseding both dogs and boats, in the more settled sections. But when we first came North, dogs and boats *were*

138

transportation, and I'm sure that no one ever thinks of Alaska even now without thinking also of Alaska's dogs.

Fall comes to Fairbanks, as Spring comes, with swift unexpectedness. The warm summer has been so real you think of it as endless, and there is no warning of a change until of a sudden there comes a frost, and then, before you know it, winter has set in. After I had summered and wintered in the North, I began to see that there were signs of coming fall, if one but noted—a wedge of geese against the sky, a regal flaunting of Queen Anne's lace. Later I learned to watch for willows and the silvery birches yellowing against the dark of spruce and tamarack; but there's no autumn here as in the south, of scarlet maple, bronze of beech or rustling russet oaks, so that first season I was unprepared for the swift change and could not understand why people urged us so to hasten and get our winter wood ordered, to have the double windows put in order and all the other preparations made for winter. Winter was unthinkable in the very midst of summer; but winter came, hardly waiting for the turn of autumnal equinox, for the last boat before the freeze-up left Fairbanks on October sixth. Then, shut within our far walled valley as we were (without the railroad that has come,

it seems, but yesterday, without the magic of to-
day's airplanes), we settled down to see just what
a northern winter meant. And to me, that first
winter meant dogs.

I had always wanted to learn to drive dogs,
and my first inquiry upon reaching Fairbanks
had been in reference to dogs, I think. And so,
before the time of earliest snowfall, my new
friends had arranged that I should meet one of
the famous dog-mushers of the North and on the
very first day of sled-snow I began my dog-mush-
ing experience. At first I was merely a passenger, and then I tried the handle-bars and
brake myself. In November I was writing home:
" I'm simply crazy about the dog teams and
have had some splendid rides as passenger already, though I plan soon to learn to drive. The
sensation when sitting in the sled and being
driven is glorious—something very like canoe-
ing; and the swift, gliding, silent motion is a
dream and an intoxication! I was out one day at
thirty below, and it is not at all unpleasant, even
then, if one is bundled. I'm going to try a small
team of five dogs first. It's a spicy team though,
let me tell you, for their names are Cinnamon,
Nutmeg, Ginger and Mace! But the leader's
name is Dan. My driver says he calls the leader
' Dan ' because it sounds so strong when you

speak it fast! How's that for ' beating the devil round the bush '? "

Now I had my first pony at the age of five, and already proudly owned two dogs, even then. I don't know when I learned to ride a horse, for it was long before that—in babyhood, I guess! I have broken and trained horses and handled various breeds of dogs for years. So to me, more important than the way the sleds were built or the harness made, was the peculiar psychology of northern dogs, differing from every other breed I've known—and for a reason. It is of that reason I wish chiefly to tell. It seemed to me then, and everything I saw and learned of northern dogs later deepened the impression, that the disposition and temperament of Alaskan dogs are their most characteristic features. Dog mushing in Alaska is a peculiar mixture of sourdough and of husky, and you can't understand dog mushing unless you know the prime quality of northern drivers and northern dogs. Dog mush ing—real *work* mushing, and not racing for record speeds—is a blend of two words: pioneer and wolf.

In the days when the Northwest was young, the Hudson Bay established a string of trading posts all through the inner land, in charge of hardy Scotch pioneers who caught and bred timber wolves for sled dogs, crossing them often with Scotch deer hounds brought from home. Even before this, for unnumbered years (at least three hundred that we know about) the Indians of the French Northwest had caught and used and partially domesticated wolves; and they still continue to cross their dogs with wolves, though whence their original wild dogs came, we do not know. From the time of the Hudson Bay, at least, the northern " work " or " sled " dog has been called a " husky " whenever the local breed runs at all true to wolf strain in color and build. The husky is larger than the " malemute "—so-called from an Eskimo tribe-name—but the two have no sharp delimits. Writers who know little of the North sometimes speak of a " thorough-bred " husky or malemute, which is of course a ridiculous misuse of words. If an Alaskan likes the look and general set-up of a dog, he'll likely call him a " husky," which is a term of respect for good qualities. If another man doesn't like the same dog's looks, or if in working he has found a yellow streak in him, he'll call the same dog " malemute," just as likely, because this word carries a certain disrespect! Both malemute and husky are prick-eared dogs, of more or less wolfish appearance. Both have bushy low-hung tails, strong legs, deep chests. Both are in gen-

eral a smoky gray in color, running to tan and
black in heads and points. Both are good servants if " kept in their place " and both are great
fighters, in the wolf manner. For the wolf strain
has been long and ever freshly bred in, and is
the continuing characteristic.

To add to the confusion of " lesser breeds without the law," ever since the white man has been
coming to the North he has been bringing with
him his own distinctive breeds of dogs, and all
of these have crossed with the true northern types
until desultory breeding has produced an amazing mixture of harness-dogs. Even among the
Eskimos there are few if any pure-bred Native
dogs to-day, except in the most remote places;
for most of the Alaskan Innuit have been in
touch with " civilization " for fifty to a hundred
years, and it doesn't take very long to change the
characteristics of a doggy generation. The Eskimo dogs, of which I've seen only one full team
of strictly genuine type, are very much smaller
than malemutes or huskies and weigh perhaps
fifty to sixty pounds, as compared with the typical malemute of one hundred to a hundred and
twenty-five. My little Eskimo friend Muk-pi
told me that her people liked little dogs, because
they " no eat so big! " But neither can they
pull " so big "—by a great deal. The bigger dog

has bigger stamina and, especially if crossed with a breed such as the famous St. Bernard, will "pull on their rep" as old-timers say. Breed will tell, as those who handle animals best know; and the fine old Alpine tradition of the passes is carrying on in the North of dogdom, among some of its non-thoroughbred but real aristocrats. This aristocratic blood-gift has been generously returned, for during the World War four thousand Alaska dogs "enlisted" and demonstrated overseas their worth, especially in the Vosges.

A cross with a good "Outside" breed will often outlast in sheer grit or character, on a grueling trail, the physically more hardened Alaskan "Native" dog. The "mongrel," just because of that half St. Bernard, or Newfoundland, or Mastiff in him, may pull on empty stomach or on bleeding feet. That's why, in most dog teams of the North to-day, you notice a strange blend of many great dog families: one has a Gordon setter look, another suggests the hound, while others still bear unmistakable hints of alien Great Dane ancestry, Airedale, or Russian Wolfhound. For much experimentation has been going on, to breed a dog for grit, endurance, speed—all three, or any one of them, according as the need arose.

But there's a surer test of "Outside" heredity

than you can get through observation, even if
you are a trained dog fancier. Use your ears,
and you'll know at once whether a dog is of an
" Inside " or an " Outside " breed, for malemutes
and huskies do not—apparently cannot—at least
they've never learned to—bark, but only howl:
the long and mournful head-thrown-back wolf
howl. That, with a little whimper of pleasure or
of eagerness, or the snarl of anger, is their whole
doggish vocabulary. The bark of the domestic
dog, with all its speaking intensity and variation
of meaning, seems to be either something he has
learned through being a human companion and
guard, or else it comes through a long ancestry
back to some other wild thing than the wolf.
Which, I do not know and cannot say. But I do
know that you cannot live long in Alaska and not
learn that malemutes and huskies howl, for they
do it singly or in discordant unison at the sight
of any full and especially glorious moon, at the
stimulus of aurora's unearthly ghost flicker, or
the sound of any steamboat whistle, church bell,
or even raised human voices. Any one of these
is quite enough to set them rearing back on their
haunches and wailing a protest to the stars!

When you live in the North, too, you must
never forget that dogs who look wolfish are very
apt to have some wolfish mental traits; and jump-

ing in a pack on any " meat " that's down or hurt or struggling, is a wolfish characteristic of ingrained instinct which only very long education will, even partially, strain out. I know of many people who, slipping and falling by accident whether in town or on the trail, were instantly attacked and torn by huskies or malemutes. It was not that the dogs were especially vicious; to attack anything that's down was merely unescapable long instinct. One little missionary at the Indian village of Chena, just below us on the Tánana, slipped and fell in the winter street and was instantly pounced on by a group of native dogs. That she fell on her face in the snow, had on a very heavy coonskin coat, and that a dozen Indian boys sprang to the rescue instantly and drove off the pack with shouts and whips, saved her life. Her coat was torn in shreds.

Handling a team of wolfish dogs, just as the handling of high-strung horses, is not at all a matter of mere physical strength. A woman can do either, and in either case she may be especially successful; but she must have that special combination of skills which belongs to the true genius of animal control, and must never, either with half-wild horse or half-wild wolf-dog, be caught off guard one moment. My experience has been that such handling calls for eternal vigilance and a deep understanding of that nervous, highly organized, temperamental animal nature. Kindness and affection and the deep-felt sentiment for animal companionship are not, in themselves, enough—though white men have in general " got more " from their dog teams, because more just, less cruel, than Natives. The truly skilled horseman will know the animal mind as he knows his very own—and know it much better than the animal himself knows it! If he does not, then there is only the great pity of a wasted power, a power without control, a vital source of energy and transportation and usefulness gone wrong for lack of a sure guiding hand. But if the human has superior understanding and superior self-control—*and* he is just—then he commands the situation, although himself physically far weaker than either powerful horse or wolf-dog pack.

When handling half-broken horses or dogs, a person who has wits will use them and not allow a situation to get out of hand. That is, he can and should but doesn't always do so, and that's just where most trouble comes. For example, all true sourdoughs know that to brush past a dog team or any group of Alaska dogs, without due warning that you are near, is to invite tragedy for which you cannot or should not blame the animals. A wolf is nervous, jumpy, on guard—for his generations are those of the wild, and he has by instinct the constant vigilance of the wild. He may seem to forget his dark forest past but, when startled, instinct swiftly speaks. And the wolf instinct cries: Snap, snatch and tear.

There is an old Russian proverb which goes: " Train a wolf as much as you like, his eyes look back to the forest." When men deliberately breed physical wolf qualities into their work dogs, they inevitably breed in also the mental qualities of wolfishness; and there are no gentle, mild, sweet-tempered and " domestic " wolves! Huskies have wolf defects as well as the greatly-to-be-desired wolf qualities. The leaders of most dog teams, the dogs you really can make pets of, are " Outside " dogs in good part. The heavy wolf-dogs are great wheelers, but they haven't usually that quick sympathy with the human voice and that quick falling in with human ways and suggestion which mark the " Outside " dog, as we know and love him. Billy's pet leader, Dan, was at least a quarter hound and a quarter mastiff, and many other good leaders have unmistakable setter or terrier points. I've never myself seen a good " wolf " *leader* in a dog team. Wolves have been wolves and have been developing their own pe-

culiar and distinctly wolfish qualities for quite
as long as men have been developing their distinctive human qualities: whereas dog breeds
have been evolved, through long use, to suit man's
purpose and fit in with his ideas of things and
living. That's why domestic dogs seem so intelligent to us, I think; for by " intelligence " we're
very apt to mean the animal's ability to adjust
himself to our own human and quick-changing
environment.

It is not fair to him, it is not safe for us, to
look upon or judge the true wolf-dog as a domestic animal. He is as wild, his nature as essentially
untamed, as many a beast now caged within a
zoo! He is a trained but an untamed wild creature—trained by man to do one trick superlatively well: pull sleds. The men who handle
wolf-dogs know this and do not make the mistake
of expecting doggy affection or doggy devotion
from a wolf. They expect and get from him
something entirely different—half-savage primitive strength, tireless ability to endure.

The genuine Alaska Pioneers have a saying
that " any one who kicks a husky should himself
be kicked twice! " When President Harding
was in Alaska and was made an honorary member of The Pioneers of Alaska, this adage was
given wide publicity by the newsmen who accom-

panied his party and it was commented on editorially all over the country. The gist of these reflections was usually in the tone of " sweetness and light," and how fine it was that Alaskans never treated their dogs cruelly. From their conclusions, these writers seemed to believe that Alaskans never punish their dogs and never use a whip! This is most false and would be not only poor justice and poor training but absolutely suicidal in any dealing with wolf-dogs. Without a whip (the symbol of control and authority, even if not used, as courts and jails are necessary symbols of authority even if they remain empty) no experienced dog musher would travel *with wolf-dogs* for a mile of trail; and he always wears his whip on a *babiche* thong over his wrist, so that he can never, even if thrown down, be separated from it for a moment. He knows better.

This law of The Pioneers, like many another code, came into being to protect the safety of the very people who made the law! It was two for the sourdoughs and one for the huskies. Why? For the same reason that most laws are not eleemosynary in motive and, like all good laws, it had its origin in fact and not in mere sentiment. A man who kicks *any* animal shows mean temper, cowardice, and a nasty disposition, and these are bad enough traits, goodness knows.

But a sourdough who kicks a wolf-dog does more. First, by the very act of kicking he puts himself off guard, off balance, and exposes a very necessary part of himself—his legs—to a pack of half-wild creatures. He's pretty nearly bound to be bitten if he does this, and bitten hard and quick! Trail mates will then have to care for him, delay their own necessary business, and perhaps suffer hardship or danger in so doing; or, if he is alone and disabled, then he is apt to die out on the trail. Some one will have to go out and hunt for him, and bring him in—if there's anything left to bring. If there isn't, then some one will have to find and kill what otherwise would have been a good and useful team of dogs, much needed for transportation in a primitive country. Half-wolves that have once tasted of revolt can never afterward be trusted not to turn on man. That's the old law of the Yukon trails, as the pioneers knew it. A rough law and a crude law, but it was law based upon savage fact.

The code of The Pioneers was not made to protect the huskies from cruelty. It was, in its essence, to protect the Arctic brotherhood itself from idiots and fools and thoughtless cowards—for a man who would kick a *chained* wolf-dog, thinking he could " get away with it," would have to deal later with the justice of the pack, when-

ever opportunity presented. The man who
kicked a husky, then, was laying up trouble for
himself and others, and the sooner he found it
out and learned " what was what," the better; and
that was why the saying spread, that " any one
who kicks a husky should himself be kicked
twice." Punishment to the erring dog should
be meted out—yes—when necessary. But not in
temper with a kick, but in clear-eyed justice, and
even then *only* with that symbol of dog law and
order and man's authority—the whip. A kick
merely shows poor sense and bad temper, and
both of these are very dangerous trail mates, to be
discouraged.

The truly amazing thing is that, being as close
to the wolf in kin as they are—so close that frequent interbreeding is common—wolf-dogs are
as " white " in spirit as they are, as generous, as
loyal, and as often kind. It's only an occasional
lapse, an occasional call of the wild, which makes
one remember how very near behind in time is,
to them, the Law of the Pack and the Dark Forest. They are of the land, as we are of it. *We*
work and trail and pack here, knowing in part our
trail-end of desire, whether it be that precious pot
at rainbow end, or golden fleece, or merely (or
best) a pioneer hearth-side in the wilderness.
They do not see our goals, they cannot sense our

far-seen aspirations, and yet they work for us
and slave for us. As Musher Brady one time
said: " Some men love dogs, and some men don't.
My Dennis, now, is the greatest leader that ever
put a neck through work-collar. Alaska! They
call it the Land that God Forgot. But we sourdoughs call it the promised land, long-sought.
We're of it, and the dogs are of it, too."

Each musher says the very same—his own is
" the greatest leader that ever put a neck through
work-collar." I've heard it scores and scores of
times. And where there is such loyalty, there's
trust. And where there's trust, then things are
getting done. That, you can wager!

All dogs are not the same, even all true Alaskan dogs. There are worlds of differences in
them. As Billy used to say, " They are just
doggy dogs, as we're just folky folks. They've
got their traits, as any collie or a setter has, as
any Cork man like myself, or any Belfast man
has traits. I've read of ' supermen,' whatever
that means. I never saw one, nor a super-dog.
These huskies have a touch of savage in them.
I like it. They're tough—that's the word—
tough. They stand the gaff, all the hard sledding. You have to, in this country, men and
dogs alike. Alaska asks it of you and you give
it—or you go.

" I've handled near a thousand dogs, belikes, in all these years, and they're a lot like folks, I find. There's a few heroes 'mongst them, and a lot fewer saints! They're mostly just like we are, tough and hardy—able to stand the trail pounding, fond of a good square meal, fond of a lively mix-up. There's no such gentleman amongst them as yon collie dog of Jack's, nor yet your Airedale, Mrs. Davis. I see your Monte walking by upon the street in Fairbanks and looking at my team of huskies, like a fine gentle-man—the kind as keeps his pants in press! His nose is tilted up, his whiskers twitch a bit, as if he's saying, ' Rough fellows, those—good chaps, no doubt, but workingmen, you know. Doubt if they know who *their* great-grand-dad was!' He has a grand aristocratic cocky way with him, that Monte dog, and holds his whiskers in the air as though he kept a monocle upon his eye, he does! Yet he's no quitter in a fight, and that I *well* know, for I've seen him at it. He fights all square and honest, and when he has his dog well licked, he will stand by just like as if he'd read his Mar-quis of Queensbury, to let the fellow take the count, all square. He doesn't make a *meal* of him, like wolves do.

" But that's not husky way of fighting—no ma'am—for they are much too near of blood to

the old wolf-sept, for anything like that. And
in *their* fighters' code, the beast that's down is
everlasting done for. I've cracked my sides
a-laughing over stories wrote by Outside men
telling of huskies sitting in a ring, like a parcel
of nice old sewing-circle ladies with their knit-
ting, a-watching two dogs fight! Say—can you
beat it! Did *you* ever see a husky that wasn't *in*
a fight, when a fight was on? No more you did,
than see an Irishman not mix it! It takes a long
trail from the wild for either dogs or humans
to learn these gentle ways, or feller feelin' for the
down-and-out, *I'm* thinking; and these huskies
is heathens—not blessed Christians, mind you.

"But, on the Devil's own trails, such as I've
seen a-plenty, they're devilish good. And I'd
be wanting no fine ' pleasure dog ' then, I would
—saving your Monte's grace!—but huskies, huskies; and the more wolf in 'em, the better I'd be
liking it."

But there is one class of Alaskan sled dogs that
is entirely different in temper and of a very different look and quality from the accepted type
of husky or malemute, and that is the Siberian.
Their use and introduction are very recent, but
they are fast becoming the most popular dog in
many mushing circles; and though they haven't
those deep roots of association with Alaska's past

and the old days which other dogs have in old-timers' minds they are, both individually and as teams, delightful to handle and phenomenally responsive. I'll never forget my own first sight of a true Siberian, for at that time no one of us in Fairbanks knew of the breed at all. This was at Teller, that little settlement on Bering Sea up beyond Nome, which was to be so startled years later when a great silver fish, frost wrapped, settled slowly out of the North sky and came to rest upon its beach—the *Norge* of Amundsen and Nobile.

This dog was of a pure white snowy fur with gray-blue, keen, alert, intelligent eyes. He was smaller than a husky but strong and lithely built and with a curled-up bushy tail—as clean and white as any Arctic fox. I loved him at first sight, and felt I could not *live* without that dog! You'll know that love-at-first-sight feeling, if you know dogs. But I could not have him, for he was a famous and beloved leader of a team, one of the first Siberians to be used in Alaska. And though I begged and pleaded, no inducements would part that dog from his master, who had tested his qualities and to whom he was dearer than any human creature, I can well believe.

These Siberians have been true-bred as sled dogs for at least five hundred years and so are truly thoroughbreds. As Seppala, the famous racer says, "Our setters, stag hounds and other kinds of dogs are pretty near perfect for the things for which they were bred; but when it comes to pulling a sled in a cold country, the Siberian is in a class by himself." Seppala was one of the first to recognize the super-quality of these immigrants from Asia. For a time, only, he made the mistake of trying to cross them with various other breeds, but he soon saw the folly of this for, as he himself admits, they're nearly perfect sled dogs already. Seppala raises his own dogs, and his choice is now this smaller, very hardy, and ever-smiling-dispositioned Siberian. No small part of his tremendous success in dog racing has been due to his pioneering insight into their superb qualities.

Siberians seem small, very small, in comparison with the great bulk of some Mastiff—or Great Dane-crossed huskies. They seem to have a trace of the fox in their ancestry and but slight, if any, trace of wolf. They have the same thick fur and strong clean-limbed set-up of the fox, and also his very bushy tail. What lends color to the fox theory, too, is that the pupil of his eye is shaped differently than is the husky's—as I believe Stefansson has commented. They are not phenomenally fast, as racers, and have not the speed of huskies crossed with hounds or other breeds; but nothing can touch them for endurance and utter dependability. They are all white or a light gray in color and are a very beautiful dog to look at, utterly responsive, and seem to delight in human friendship, contacts and control. So far as I have ever heard, they haven't even a trace of wolfish treachery in their makeup. In fact, though in physique a perfect sled dog, in temper they are a perfect "pleasure dog" and companion.

But when you've mentioned Leonhard Seppala, you've brought to mind the whole saga of "The Glory Trail," the All Alaska Sweepstakes. And dog racing belongs to another chapter in Alaska's story.

X

Dog Derby and Ice Pool

Can you remember your huskies all going,
  Barking with joy and their brushes in air—
You in your parka, glad-eyed and glowing?
                                        SERVICE.

IN the Valley of Paradox which is Interior
  Alaska, spring can be either our dullest or
most dramatic season! During November, December and January we have had none of the
actinic rays of sun for tonic, and the piled-up
effect of all these months tends to key our people
nervously—to make us, as the spring approaches,
tense and scratchy and irritable. One man says
that after the long dark months " the everlasting
sun makes me nervous! " Little frictions that
would be meaningless at other times, now as-
sume immense proportions. Stefansson tells of
one lifelong friendship turned to enmity during
this period of high tension, because " *Some*body
got up in the dark and ate a quarter of a pound
of chocolate! " What brittle pal-ships I've seen
snapped in the electric surcharged air of late
winter and early spring! Partners so angry of

a sudden at each other, that they decide like
quarrelsome children to " split the blanket " then
and there, and start in blind unreason to divide
everything—even to cutting a boat in half.

One miner tells that he saw " a coupla fellows
even breakin' up their *stove* in two! "   Another
sourdough put it this way: " Come along spring,
the moccasin racks of the old-timers begins to
itch.   And it ain't from unjumped socks, neither.
You want to feel the trail again under a shoe-
pac."   Jumped socks?   They're one of the old
sourdough's best housekeeping devices, for he
doesn't pack a darning needle in his kit.   When
a hole appears in the heel of his thick, shapeless,
woolen socks he merely turns them about or
" jumps " them, and keeps on turning or jump-
ing the hole to places where it doesn't hurt his
foot, until the lower sock has worn away entirely.   Then he sews up the top, makes a toe of
that, and jumps the sock once more.   Six
" jumps " is a good record, even for sourdough
socks!

In the towns, of course, there are many go-
ings-on in winter, for that is our real social get-
together season.   We have our Scout Troops,
our D.A.R. Chapters, and all the various lodges
known Outside, as well as The Pioneers of
Alaska—an association open to those who have

Photograph by Lomen Brothers.

"ALL HE ASKS IS A RAFT, AND THE ARCTIC ICE-FLOES PROVIDE THAT."

Photograph by Lomen Brothers.

WALRUS AMONG THE ICE-FLOES IN BERING SEA NEAR NOME.

Photograph by Lomen Brothers.

REINDEER ARE SOMETIMES USED FOR DRIVING.

Photograph by Lomen Brothers.

SNOW DOES NOT INTERFERE WITH REINDEER PASTURE.

been in the Territory a certain number of years
—and The Native Sons and Daughters of the
Golden North, to which white children born in
Alaska or Yukon Territory are eligible. We
have a splendid movie theatre, club houses,
churches, women's clubs. Even in the old days
of over-the-ice eggs and " Rocky Mountain Ice
Cream " made of powdered milk and dessicated
eggs, there were parties and dinners and all
manner of social activities, galore. The very lack
of many household " necessities," then, was a
challenge to our pioneering ingenuity and
spurred us housekeepers to unusual efforts. No
lettuce after November? Then we used begonia
leaves to decorate our tasty gelatine winter
salads, because they looked so glossy green.
No fresh lemons in the local stores after
January? Very well, then, we will buy a case
of lemons in the fall, put them in the outdoor cache at the moment of the first deep
cold in November, and when we need a lemon
merely fetch one in, dip it in scalding water and
use immediately—or slice it thinly, already
frozen, for our tea. This served our every purpose, we had the fun of discovering it for ourselves, and felt like Newton watching the apple
fall or Watt with one eye on the kettle spout!
We rolled out great spicy stacks of temptingly

odorous mince pies in November. I say "stacks" because I mean real stacks! For we piled those pies neatly in the cache, with a piece of oiled paper in between, froze them solidly instanter at 40° below zero, and whenever we would have a pie thereafter we merely nicked one loose with the ice-pick, popped the pie into the oven—and feasted.

From my own experience, I'd say that our main peril in the "Frozen North" in winter was from overeating! You crave sweets in great quantity during the deep cold, for your body shouts to you to feed it *fuel;* so fats and sugars are the things you fall upon most greedily and you are rather apt to overdo it. The sourdough's sweet-tooth has dug many an early grave, I fear. But such good times we had, even in those winters before the railroad made housekeeping easy! Shut in together through the long winter months, we came to know both the highest and the lowest traits in one another, through mutual experiences inextricably woven. And there were afternoon calls by brilliant winter moonlight, and there was skating on Noyes' Slough in early fall before the snow came, or on the skating rink up by the Signal Corps where the boys rigged a flood light and played hockey, Hallowe'en or on Alaska Day.

In summer, there were fish in all the streams, motors on the many woodland roads, sailboats on Harding Lake. Summer evenings are game and picnic times, in this land of soft midnight color with blue and purple shadows on the hills, flowers in wide masses and profusion and fields of rufous fox-tail and magenta fire-weed on the " burn-off." Owl baseball is played here by daylight; the tennis courts are most popular from ten P. M. to two A. M. for then the sunlight is most soft. One of our Alaska bishops says: " Alaska may not *be* heaven but it's a lot *like* it! You go up to get there, only those may stay here who have passed certain tests of character, there is no night here, and moths don't corrupt—though one may admit a *little* rust! Yet there are no snakes in the land. Saint Frost, like another Saint Patrick, rid us of them, long ago."

It's spring, not summer or winter, when the North most presses in on one, the sense of isolation from the outer world becomes most keen, the restlessness of an inactive winter (when our frozen mines can't be worked) comes upon the men, unbalanced diet begins to tell as well as lack of normal exercise during the severe cold; and on the creeks there is that close confinement in too narrow quarters with companions—gay at first—who have perhaps become uncongenial or boresome, now. Then, too, the Earth is a great magnet and near its poles we feel the full effect of electricity in atmosphere. All this tells on our nerves and makes us scratchy. By the end of March I think we might well be avoiding and hating one another—if we had not thought up ways to draw off all this electric surcharge, into harmless and interesting channels. That's why we stage our two dramatic spring events, the dog derby and the ice pool. When the days begin to lengthen, when the men of the North get restless and begin milling around, then we start talking sweepstakes and every one is happy once again.

Dogs are not only a work necessity but a social asset here, and the Northern dog is now going through a transition very like that of horses recently in the States. Once the dog was a vital necessity for work and cartage but now he is becoming, especially in our Northern springtime, a symbol of true social elegance! To " put on dog " in Fairbanks means that you own or back or drive an especially bred, trained, and picked racing team in the Dog Derby. It's all quite as sporting a proposition as polo or horse racing.

So much has been told of Nome's great " Glory Trail " and the famous old All-Alaska Sweepstakes of the early days, that I'll need only

to remind you of it here.   Late in spring when
the days were long and the trail was hard, the
course was set from Nome to Candle and return
—408 miles of strength, speed, endurance, courage and good judgment.   The course was over
treeless tundra from Bering Sea to the Arctic
Ocean and return—over the Topkok Divide to
Council City, along Fish River to Death Valley,
across and down Kiwalik River to Candle Creek
and return—74 hours and 18 minutes! Icy coast
—the long mush—often a blinding blizzard that
made a curtain of horizontal sleeted snow—that's
sport of the type which eats your oxygen and
breaks the heart of any dog or man with the
vaguest trace of yellow.

The formalities of the race and its traditions
were ancient and rigid.   Every dog must be
registered at the start and every driver must return with the same dogs, dead or alive.   The
All-Alaska Sweepstakes caused exactly the same
emotions and excitement in Alaska that the
World Series does in eastern cities, and frosty
Nome cries " Seppala " to-day, when the Borden
Marathon is being run, as in other places the
name of Cobb or Ruth or Walter Johnson has
been shouted.   Nome is frozen in from November often until July, and without her many dog
races, beginning with the " burden race " on

Washington's Birthday, Nome people would go half mad with impatience in the long-delaying springtime.

We of Fairbanks have also our spring dog races early in March, and although our winters are usually less trying and our spring more swift in coming, we too are all agog with the wholesome spring excitement over our great event, which we call the Dog Derby. We have a lively Kennel Club, dedicated to " the recognition, perpetuation, and improvement of the Alaskan dog," and our District Judge owns one of our best racing teams and plunges with the rest of us in lively anticipation of good sport, the racers assembling at the Court House and there drawing for place. We eat, sleep and talk dogs, for weeks. A good race-dog costs $250, a fine leader $1,200; and as the teams run from seven up, you'll see it's not a " piker's " game! " Who will win the Derby? " is the big question—Charlie Brink's steady and heavy Iditarod huskies, Judge Clegg's matched light Siberians, Jake Mutchler's Tacotna wolves, the malemutes of Joe Stickman the lame Indian boy from Nulato, or " Sig Wigg's grayhounds? " Fifty-eight miles of rough road, with a steep summit to climb, are ahead of them. Our newspaper begins its " Dog Dope " column in January, and by February we hear nothing but dog—

truly! If howling made success they'd all be
winners, for the February moon is full of wolf
music. The other night the fire siren blew while
we had our 497 guest dogs here for the races—
and shades of Wagner, what a chorus!

" If there's one thing more uncertain than a
horse race, it's a dog race," the trail blazer is saying. " There's no better way to satisfy yourself
just what kind of a bunch of dogs you been
a-feedin' all winter, than by backin' 'em agin
what the other fellow's got." Substitute
" horse " for " dog " in the run of early spring
conversation about Fairbanks, and you might as
well be in Louisville or Bowie or Havre de
Grace! Visiting dog teams begin to appear in
town during early February, and they are invariably a rallying point of interest for all dog-
wise old-timers, who inspect with shrewd and
knowing eyes and issue sage pronouncements
about their chances of " being in the money."

Some of our visiting teams have never smelt a
" gas wagon," since they have come from road-
less river villages. So all motorists are asked, in
courtesy and good sport, not to be on the road
for several hours before the races. Joe Ulmer,
blazer of trails, just phoned in from Summit to
say that the course was flagged and staked, all
ready for the big day. The latest gossip is that

teamsters of the Road Commission hitched a string of dead rabbits behind a sled yesterday and dragged the whole course, " to pep up the pups! " And every plane in town is engaged, to take " real sports " aloft to see the race from air. Word of an accident in which a dog's leg has been broken, is sometimes received during the race and causes great commotion; for by the rules each dog, dead or alive, must be brought back. " Will he make it, with that handicap? " New wagers must be laid.

Who can remember now that winter is too long, or that we are a little far-off settlement removed from all the world? No one has time to get a " spring grouch " or spring indigestion, during this excitement. Our little colony is all speeded up, a-dog with pep, " rarin' to go " and wild to win. I'm sure that we in Fairbanks, during the trying and nerve-tense spring, are happier and healthier people, thanks to the good dogs and the good clean sport that mark for us the break of winter.

We have no sooner recovered from the howls, yelps and thrills of the races than we begin to wonder when the ice will move in the river. And the moment an Alaskan begins to wonder he begins to act, for purely philosophic contemplation of events is not a part of any Alaskan's make-up! He wants a stake in anything that's doing and so, ever since 1903, there has been great wagering of judgment against judgment on the day, hour and minute when the tight-packed ice on the Tánana will move. By now, the exact moment of that first move has been reduced to scientific accuracy. But this is how my good friend Meta Bloom, who was born here and is one of our active Fairbanks Girl Scouts, describes the excitement of the break-up:

" Year in, year out, the mighty waters of the Tánana River flow peacefully between its banks from May till November. From November until May it is bound by a six-foot-thick blanket of snow-covered ice. This blanket is not entirely useless. Roads are cleared upon it, over which conveyances ranging from dog teams to heavily-loaded wood sleds drawn by strapping horses, travel all winter long. Rinks are also cleared on it by enterprising groups of skating enthusiasts. People do not permit this covering to deprive them of the full use of the river. Holes are drilled to the surface of the water, and ice, fish, and the winter's water supply are acquired in this way.

" However, there comes a time when signs appear on the banks and notices in the daily paper to the effect that skaters and others shall keep off the ice because it is rapidly softening and the break-up may be expected any minute now.

" Then the break-up arrives. The cry, ' The ice is going out!' rings through the town and the entire able-bodied population are on the banks of the river in less time than it takes to tell.

"Ah, but it is an impressive sight! The ice breaks into various sized chunks, some broad enough for a large house to rest upon, others so minute that they are hardly discernible. However, big or little, they are all bound in one direction, down river toward the sea, perhaps impelled in that direction by the long-suffering river now rapidly rising between its banks, perhaps taking pity on it for its long imprisonment and anxious to set it free.

"Many and varied are the objects seen floating on the chunks; tin cans and other refuse, whole trees, trunks and branches complete; and one memorable break-up, a live cat was seen riding to its doom atop a cake of ice.

"Often after the break-up, the river gaily overflows its banks and floods the first few streets of the town; however, I can only remember two such occasions—one being when I was very young, and the other this year of grace, 1929.

"So much for the break-up. Though it is a magnificent and awe-inspiring sight, though it heralds the coming of the short but glorious Alaska summer, though it allows the resumption of river traffic and river fishing, it is for us Fairbanksans merely a means toward an end, that end being the ice pool!

"About the time that the river ice begins to become dangerously soft, a pole is erected on a prominent spot on the ice, near the bridge. A sign bearing the name of the town's most popular café is placed on top of the pole. This is connected by electric wiring to an electric clock in this same café, and when the ice moves, the pole moves, the wire breaks, the current is stopped, and the clock stops. The whole thing hinges on the time this clock stops. Bets are laid, often totaling seventy-five thousand dollars; people bet, or more genteel folks 'guess,' on the minute, on the hour, on the day—each one separately or all three together.

"Every one has it down pat. They produce statistics to prove it. They could not possibly miss it. This is the time when the miser and the philanthropist meet on equal terms. Each one spends his dollars with equal abandon. Then when the fatal day arrives and your arch-enemy, who is rich as Crœsus already, wins the entire pool, including your hard-earned dollars—you are through, through with aimless uncalculated betting, through with foolish squandering, through with the whole blooming (other more forceful adjectives may be substituted) lay out. Never again, no sir, never— until the *next* break-up!"

But the Dog Derby and the Ice Pool are not our only sports. In winter, many people in Fairbanks have great sport at the Curling Club, and the Beef and Greens Dinner of this club is one of the real events of the year. We have also High School, College, Town and "All Star" basket-ball teams, and now that winter intercourse is possible between Fairbanks and the Coast, the High School team last year went on tour to the Coast and won its laurels there—won the championship in both Interior Alaska and Railroad Belt Leagues, and only lost the All-Alaska championship to Petersburg in the last three minutes of their third game. During base-ball season we are very busy people here at bread and butter doings, but we have a ball team and there are always several good games during the summer, for as "W. F." our editor put it: "Diamond dust *must* be made!" No summer solstice celebration is complete without a midnight ball game at the park for, like all far northern peoples, midsummer night means much to us and is a real festival.

June twenty-first, at ten P. M. the umpire cries "Play ball," and ball is played until some time between twelve and two A. M. It is an immemorial part of our midsummer festival. Then as we go to have a snack at midnight, before the gay costume ball which every one, young and old, attends, we look up in the clear blue sky and see the filmy shadow of a lemon-tinted moon, a lonely ghost in heaven. It's here we learn that sleeping "nights" is merely a habit—convenient only because in most places "night time" means dark, and the impossibility of outdoor work or recreation. But ours is the true Festival of the Midnight Sun.

Old "W. F." (a-limp back from the ball park on that foot he wrecked in a tri-league ball game on Ocean Beach, in the Gray's Harbor country years ago) looks up at that pale yellow slip of moon and squints one eye at her and one at me, and says: "Now, ain't God good to Fairbanks?" He is, and well we know it.

Then, too, Alaskans have two extra, special and peculiar holidays that are all our very own. It's like two birthdays in each year and because Alaska's so young she doesn't mind having two! Besides, being of Russian birth, Alaska is entitled to the Greek Church custom of two birthdays in a year—an actual age-day and a patron-saint day. The 30th of March is Seward Day and commemorates that early morning hour in 1867 when Seward and the Ambassador of Russia, Baron Stoeckl, after working all night upon the draft of a treaty ceding Alaska to the U. S. A., finally put their seals to the momentous document with a sigh of relief and joy. And " Alaska Day," October 18, commemorates the formal transfer of Alaska to Uncle Sam's ward and tutelage, and is always celebrated by a formal holiday all over the Territory. If " a people are known by the holidays they keep," as a wit once said, then Alaskans should be known as mighty good and loyal Americans, for our two especially honored feast-days are those which celebrate—not independence from, but our *de*pendence on, our Uncle Sam.

XI

High Pass and Low Divide

Who hath smelt wood smoke at twilight? Who hath
    heard the birch log burning?
Who is quick to read the voices of the night?
Let him follow with the others, for the Young Men's
    feet are turning
To the camps of proved desire and known delight.
                           KIPLING.

IN early days, when Fairbanks was just another new raw gold camp, the Yukon was
the one sure summer trail to reach it, by boat
from Nome or down from Klondike and thence
up-river on the Tánana. In winter, one could
travel too by sled upon the River, coming down
from Dawson and cutting across country to Fairbanks (" The Tánana Camp," as old-timers always called it) at the point where the two rivers
began to wedge together. This was the " over-
the-ice " way, used by many.

Soon after gold was found in quantity in this
section, however, the United States Army began
to be interested in more direct overland routes
to the Interior, because a new influx of settling

whites always meant plenty of Indian problems. A rough trail was broken out across the coast ranges from the Pacific at Valdez, and called by prospectors " The All-American Route." Later, when very rich copper lodes were found at Kennecott on upper Copper River behind Cordova, New York capital built a railroad up along that treacherous richly scenic river, past monster glaciers, to fetch out the red ore, (as you well know if you have read Rex Beach's thrilling story of that venture, " The Iron Trail "), and a branch of the newly developing military road to Fairbanks was made to tap this railroad at Chitina.

Now we had two land routes to Fairbanks; and to-day, over that once rough mountain trail blazed out in risk and peril, there runs an excellent graveled auto road from Fairbanks down to Valdez or to Chitina. This Richardson Trail was for many years the one winter link between us Interiorites and all the rest of the world. Along it, too, were strung those copper threads of the Signal Corps' Telegraph Line—" wire talk," the Natives called it—across which we could greet our friends so far away.

But summer freight by the long boat-haul, up from San Francisco or Seattle to St. Michael at the Yukon's mouth and thence by clumsy barges pushed the weary miles up-stream, was desperately slow work. Winter freight over the trail from the Coast, in horse-drawn double-ender sleds across the passes, was slow work, too, and most expensive—even for the only possible smallest express pieces and first-class mail. We knew that the wide West was never really won as great states and true homelands, until a railroad pushed across those empty miles. And we knew, too, that here in our great Middle North we had a similar Land of Promise, if only there could be a steel trail blazed, from ocean harbor on the southern coast to tap the dormant richness of the gravid Yukon-Tánana Valley.

After years of talk and waiting and sick hearts from hope deferred, at last the railroad came and now makes all-year-round communication between The Tánana Camp and open sea water, at Seward and Anchorage. In the one month of December, 1929, this railroad bought and paid for 5,000 tons of Alaska's Healy River fuel, for it opens into coal fields as well as gold fields. The Alaska Railroad has indeed already proved the one truly generous and most appreciated gesture which Uncle Sam has made toward his North—a monument to-day, in ribboned steel, to a far-sighted policy of true development in this most new and northern empire.

I came over the route of that railroad, before ever it was built, in winter and with dogs. The snows were so deep on the south side that for days we walked upon the *tops* of trees, and any little misstep sent our sleds spinning down into the inverted cones of snow about the submerged conifers. That was the old way of winter travel —days of labor and effort to make a few miles, in deep snows and in constant peril of avalanche while mushing through the steep mountain gulches. In one day we were caught in three such slides, and only by the greatest luck came out of them with our whole skins. Now you can travel year round over that same mountain trail in Pullman observation coaches! That's why we say that no one not living here before the railroad came, will ever even guess what it has meant to us who were, before its coming, merely far frontiersmen. Now we are colonists, for we have a road, a railroad, a river way and the new air way, to take us from the Golden Heart and its wheat-growing gold-washed valley of the Inner Lands whenever we must make a trip Outside, or to bring travelers here who wish to see the beauty of the summer North. The winters— which many of us Northmen think the best of seasons—the tourists seldom care to see.

The very central boss of that great mountain

barrier between us and the Coast, now pierced by
rail and road, is Mount McKinley, rising nearly
four miles high. It is not only the highest peak
in North America, but highest mountain summit
in the world *above its surrounding base,* for it
rises sheer from a low valley floor in truly un-
believable majesty. Small wonder that the
Indians of these central lands, looking up to it,
spoke of Denali, " The Most High," or called it
amongst themselves in their rich picture language, " The Last Home of the Sun." From the
south windows of our Fairbanks home we looked
out on that mountain daily, the great peak rising
clear and gleaming like a giant opal in the clean
sub-arctic air, although a hundred and fifty miles
away as crows fly. It called, and called. And
long before the railroad had been built, I had the
rare good luck to be (as Fannie Quigley said I
was, and she had lived for many years near to the
mountain's base in " the Kantish'na country,"
and must have known) the first white woman to
mush over to its foot and back by some newly
found passes through the very center of the continent's backbone. That was a real adventure,
and Fannie herself was not the least of it. She
is a Klondike sourdough, a famous shot, a most
observant big-game hunter, a trapper, a prospector, a magic cook, and the best good company

that any one could wish. I stayed with her
eleven days, in her wee cabin clinging to steep
mountain slope, and living with Fannie is like
being *in* a story book!

This mush of ours was made during late
August and early September, but there were already heavy snows in the high passes. In the
lower valleys the early autumn glory was upon
the land, the silver birch a flame of golden yellow,
the spruce trees black in shadow but glowing
green when washed in sun, the flaming high red
of the million-berried cranberry brush weaving
a tapestry of warm full color. And all the birds
—" the summer people," as the Tinneh Indians
fondly call them: warblers and robins, tree sparrows and the tow and red heads of the gros-
beaks, chickadees in flocks, many a thrush at
dawn, goshawk and widgeon overhead, wood-
pecker busy at his spruce-trunk grubbing—
Tokoroldala, Indians call him, such a flowing
name! Willows and cottonwoods upon the
meandering river flats, open spaces in the pockets
rich in grass, and a red fox streaking across, all
but his black stockings and white tip of thick-
furred brush a flame and flash of autumn color;
chatter of squirrels preparing larders for the
winter, ducks and blackbirds in a clustered flight,
jabber of jays. And in the night, rolled up upon

the earth and listening to the night sounds—the eerie whoo-whoo of the ghostly great horned owl, or to the little owl that catches mice at night and which the Indians call " The-thing-that-perches-on-the-lower-branches-of-the-spruce-trees." They surely use long words, for little birds! But the small fellow is spirit of a shaman, Natives say; and listening in the dark, I did not wonder that witchcraft and moon-shadowed spruce woods ever belong together.

We " siwashed " on this mushing trip—that is, slept out, as Natives do. The early French trappers called living as a Native does " sauvage " or savage life, and so to this day primitive Alaskan camping means to " Siwash." But one night there was something more than eerie hoot of owl, to startle. We were almost asleep, in a shelter of spruce just below timber line, when suddenly our pack-horses staked out near-by began to snort and snuff, pull at their ropes and, when we went to see what we could see, we found them tugging at their pickets in wild panic, staring as we did, wide-eyed in the dark but seeing nothing. Black clouds of coming snow hid our small moon, and all was deepest shadow. But something crackled in the brush occasionally, and though our stupid human noses could not catch the odor, we knew from the stiff primitive terror of the horses that *they* smelled bear. For nothing will so panic them.

But we knew what would startle Mr. Bear—a trick that man had learned long ages since but which the beasts have never caught the knack of. A lone spruce, dry of leaf and with a few dead lower branches, stood apart from our camp shelter. We found it in the open dark, drew out our magic man-box and scratched a little stick along its side. A new, low flickering star came out and this we touched to those dead lower branches of the spruce. In a split second, flames roared into the sky with a million spreading sparks. Each dry spruce tip rose in a rush of rocket-soaring fire, a glorious pyre against black thickness of the night. We stood and watched, like children at a magic show, until the last glow died and all was pitch again.

We stole back to the horses, speaking softly not to startle them. But they were grazing, now, and quiet. The thing which prowled had left—for keeps—when their man-god had made his magic for them. They knew, now, they were safe.

Such grand good feasts of ptarmigan we had! Brush brown in summer and snow white in winter, now they were well advanced in change to winter plumage, with only a dark throat-piece left. Bunching up for early winter they were easy enough good meat for " siwashers," and breasts of fall-fat ptarmigan are " easy eating!" In the early mornings we could hear them chatter in flocks about our higher snow blown camps, clucking and calling like so many barnyard hens a-feeding. And in the lower camps were willow or ruffled grouse, the smaller " drummer " whose flesh is all white when cooked. Sometimes we saw a sharp-tailed grouse—the one the Indians call *Toledoya* or " the sitter," a metaphor which any old prairie-chicken hunter will appreciate. The dark spruce hen or partridge is *Ala'ona,* " The spruce-eater " because of her winter diet of needles. Observant eyes, these Natives!

In our part of Alaska we have few if any true singing birds in winter, for the songsters are mostly summer tourists. With early spring come the wild ducks and snow geese, while the Emperor goose or " hooded one " moves north from the Aleutians to the Bering Sea. Camp robber jays have stayed all winter, the little scamps; but many of the other birds are migratory, and those leg-banded here have been " read " in far-away Australia, France, and South America. As soon as snow has gone come red-breasts bursting with their song, the blue-birds, sparrows, swallows. Finches, cranes and swans, gulls, plovers, thousands of eider-duck and hopping, twittering snow-bunting are found very much further north even than we live—up to the exotic, silver-traced and myriad-colored mosses of the Northern Slope, where you'll find foxes nest-hunting on the tundras; and I imagine those same foxes can give account for many an Alaskan pipit and ptarmigan. The summer Arctic is a vast bird-haunt, while round the lakes of Alaska's peninsulas and moose ponds full of lily pads and muskrats, are many shrikes and jays, cross-bills and three-toed woodpeckers, even though nesting migratory fowl pay tithe to wolves and coyotes, and geese are most especially heavy sufferers.

We have found wolves numerous over nearly all Alaska, even up to the Arctic Slope where the Eskimo white wolf of a creamy color, *ki-gi-lún-uk,* ranges from Bering Straits all the way across to the Atlantic, so I'm told, and one of the Eskimo words for white man *is* " white wolf." Over the rest of the land ranges the common big gray timber wolf, the *" loup gris "* of the early Frenchmen and the progenitor of many an Alaskan sled dog. Some one has truly said, " The wolf is a wild dog, the dog is an honest wolf." Wolves do great damage to stock and game in Alaska and during the past year, five

wolves killed more than 500 reindeer near
Unalakleet, and two wolves killed 200 near St.
Michael—40 within a few days' time, much more
than they could possibly eat.   Not only do they
commit their depredations on sheep and caribou
and moose, thus greatly cutting down man's
natural meat supply, but they are death to many
valuable fur bearers, too—to foxes and beaver,
especially—as well as all the toll of all that they,
with wolverines and bears, steal from prospectors, miners, and trappers.

One of the cleverest of all the hunting tricks
which Chick-em the Eskimo hunter told me, was
" the old way " in which his people used to catch
a wolf.   Some, of course, were killed with
arrows, and some in traps.   But wolves are hard
to see—in all my years of West and North,
though I have spent many a night on the prairie
listening to their close howl and near-by circling
and have seen a thousand wolf-torn animals, I've
only seen two wild wolves close by.   And Lupus
is very trap wise.

Knowing this, the canny Eskimo hunter made
slender splints of whalebone about nine inches
long, a quarter of an inch wide, and pointed them
sharply at each end.   These he softened until he
could bend them back upon themselves in spring-
wise folds only a couple of inches long, and bound

them tightly in this position with a cord, until thoroughly dry. Then Chick-em took the cord off, soaked the coiled whalebone bundle well in oil to remove all " man-smell," wrapped it up in a fat hunk of blubber or fish, and put it in some conspicuous place on a wolf trail, handling it only with forked sticks.

Mr. Wolf sees it, smells it, finds it quite to his liking. Then he begins to eat, but finding it very tough, swallows it whole, dog fashion—thinking it gristle, I imagine. But when the whalebone becomes warm in Lupus' tummy and moist with his digestive juices, it straightens out to its full nine-inch length again and its deadly barbed ends pierce the beast's stomach. A cruel trick, perhaps, but the Arctic hunter wins his meat and fur in a cruel land. Lupus himself has lived long by his wits, was never dainty in his kill, and shows no mercy.

In the Kantishna, our entire trek lay through most marvelous game country. Before we started, Harry Karstens told us: " There's no place in the world where mountain sheep are so plentiful. There are thousands of them, over there." I thought this a great exaggeration, for I believed (as do most people) that these almost pure white Dall's sheep (the Alaska cousin of the famous Big Horn family) are relatively rare

game animals. I thought, " I'll just see for myself. Hunters and explorers tell big stories."
So I took with me a " tin ticker " or sheep
counter, such as men use in the West for making
a sheep or cattle tally, at shearing-time or
round-up. The first three days of the trek into
the hills I kept this constantly in my hand, and
every time I saw a mountain sheep I punched
the record. But we saw such bands of them—
all over the mountain slopes, bands of 75 to 150
each—by that third night my " ticker " registered over 1,000 already, and I quit counting!
I cannot truly say how many we saw, for I
stopped recording at 1,000 even though I had
sworn an oath to keep it—on the horns of *Ovis
dalli,* even as Kipling swore upon the horns of
Ovis poli! For our Alaskan Big Horns were
named for Dall (the scientist of the old Western
Union survey back in the sixties) by his friend
Dr. E. W. Nelson, just as those of the Pamir
Plateau were named for Marco Polo who met
them in the thirteenth century.

Many people think the white mountain sheep
is a goat; but it isn't, even though it may suggest an American ibex! It is larger than the
largest domestic sheep, and stoutly built. Both
sexes wear horns and those of the rams are
greatly curved and heavy, with a decided ridge

for every year of the animal's age.   I'm told by
old hunters that about fifty inches, measured
around the outside curve from base to tip, is a
record, though horns will shrink somewhat after
drying. Perfect mountain sheep horns with
unbroken tips are very rare. Charles Sheldon,
who made a life study of them, thought that these
horns rub on the rocky ground as the animal
feeds and that breakage came from the shock of
head-on combat when the rams fight; for they
are batters!

I came up over a sharp ridge, one day in the
Kantishna country, to find two large rams staring me full in the face, not fifty feet away. They
were the very picture of un-fear, at home on their
high hills, poised, alert, interested, one fore foot
slightly raised, one hind foot lightly poised in
the fine snow—as untense, relaxed and confident
as a cayuse upon western range. They did not
hurry off but took a good long look at me, and I
at them. Some hunters say, these sheep always
graze looking *down* their mountain, for that's the
way that any danger comes; so that in hunting
you can get the best shot from above—if you can
get above, for they've good eyes and scent! And
if there is a place that's snowy or " glaciered "
(the word Alaskans use for frozen over, overflow) " then you can slide them down right into

camp, after you've shot 'em, and save yourself a long hard pack. And when you skin 'em out, take a low cut for the cape, so's when you taxiderm it, the head will show the bulge of the shoulder. Give the cape a good dose of salt, after scraping all the fat off, and in this climate that's a-plenty to keep it sweet indefinite, until you want to tan it right."

Going up one long black gulch, on our way over to Denali, three grizzlies followed us all afternoon on the ridge just above, and not a quarter mile away. One of them, the mother, was a giantess. I wish I knew how big she really was, but we had only a twenty-two and so were very careful not to " start anything! " Near Fairbanks we have plenty of friendly, curious black bears—" The-little-one-who-walks-apart " of the Natives, or " The-one-living-under-the-steep-hill." The Tinneh call these black bears, too, " The-elder-brother-of-the-porcupine " and grizzlies, such as those that followed us, they will sometimes call " The-elder-brother-of-the-black-bear."

All kinds of bears are here, and grizzlies are quite too plentiful over nearly all Alaska. They are of all colors, from almost white to almost black, ranging through yellows, tans and browns —though the most characteristic grizzly, so old hunters say, is the famous silver-tip. They have been measured nine feet long—and those not measured were all longer! Scientists distinguish between the grizzly with its subspecies, and the Big Brown; " but it's hard for ordinary people to tell them apart." Petrof of the 1880 Alaska census tells of a Kodiak brown bear that measured fourteen feet four inches; but these Alaskan Kodiaks are the largest carniverous animals extant, " high as a cow—much larger than a lion."

The heaviest authentic weight I've heard for a grizzly is 1,153 pounds. They are much fiercer than the common black bear and are really the only wild animal of Alaska forests which the Natives fear. Indians almost never sought an encounter with *Tlaruza;* and to this day, when going through a wood where he is known to live, will sing or beat a drum or a tin can, " to tell him we are coming." This is considered " more polite "—and also *much* more safe! A startled grizzly is not a pleasant trail experience, for any one. But the Tinneh were far from cowards, for the old-time Indian way to kill a grizzly, when that was necessary, was to spear it through the heart with a ten-inch copper dagger lashed to a short pole—*after* the great beast had reared to grapple with you at arms' length! That is too close for me! I much prefer a high-powered rifle and long range.

The Eskimos, too, are very polite about bears. They call the polar bear by high-sounding names of praise, and if a man makes sport of any bear or calls him disrespectful names, the bears will all watch for him on the trail and kill him, Chick-em says. A bear hunter starting out will make a flowery oration, speaking in greatest respect and reverence of all bears, and especially of the one he hopes to kill! "I go kill seal," he says, or "I go now, kill wolf"—or fox, or any other creature. This "puts the bear to sleep." No Eskimo hunter likes to speak of what he plans to kill when he goes hunting, and for this reason some whites have called them liars. It's really only hunter's caution. If you speak of your intention, they believe the animals will hear and know, and you will surely have bad luck.

But we were not bear hunting in Kantishna, although it seemed at times as though they hunted us. In one day we saw five, and no day was bearless—if you count that bear the horses smelled but we could not. Even when we could not see them, we knew they saw and followed us. When I was not counting Big Horns, I kept my eyes open for those five-toe-and-a-palm marks of the grizzly, with deep scratchy nail-points made by those long, slender, straightened fore claws.

For " horribilis " and " grizzly " are not comfortable words—now, are they?—with all the connotation which they carry of the gruesome, grim and terrible. And yet I know that the grizzly is mostly herbivorous, living on grasses, roots, mushrooms and wild berries or, for variety, on honey and fish, and birds' eggs—or, for a change again when a square meal is needed, on any animal from mouse to moose. I've seen them in the salmon streams and berry patches in late summer or, other times, digging for mice, ground squirrels or roots. As John Muir says, " His bread is sure, ranged on the shelves of the mountains like stores in a pantry. From one to another, from climate to climate, up and down he climbs, feasting on each in turn, enjoying as great variety as if he traveled to far-off countries, north and south. To him, almost anything is food—except granite! Every tree helps to feed him, every bush; and herbs, with fruits, flowers, leaves and bark . . . crunched and hashed, down all go to this marvelous stomach, and vanish as if cast into a fire. What digestion! "

To-day they're saddling those " humps," as Fannie called our Sable Mountain, Polychrome, Highway and Far Pass. They're building a fine

tourist's motor road along those gulches which
we ventured, over those passes, and Fannie
Quigley's still unravished quietness will soon be
lost to her.   Last year a thousand travelers
drove by automobile to within four miles of Tok-
lat, to touch the very skirt of distance and the
far-to-seek.   Soon they will be at Copper Mountain, Muldrow Glacier, Wonder Lake and the
great massif's very footstool where once we stood
and worshipped The Most High, our heads
thrown back to catch the glory of an early sun
upon that heaven-piercing summit.

Perhaps, then, pioneering Fannie will move a
further league or so within the sheltering hills,
and so too will my curious grizzly friends.   *They*
will not relish scent of gas, or rubber imprint on
their valley floor.   But with a growl and a roar
—or maybe just a sniff or cough or one deep-
chested grunt—they'll look, and turn, and go.

XII

Around the Moons with Muk-pi

The People of the Eastern Ice, they are melting like
    the snow—
They beg for coffee and sugar; they go where the
    white men go.
The People of the Western Ice, they learn to steal
    and fight;
They sell their furs to the trading post; they sell their
    souls to the white.
The People of the Southern Ice, they trade with the
    whaler's crew;
Their women have many ribbons, but their tents are
    torn and few.
But the People of the Elder Ice, beyond the white
    man's ken—
Their spears are made of the narwhal-horn and they
    are the last of The Men!

KIPLING.

I HAD a very dear Eskimo friend. That small
word " had " can be so packed with sadness,
but I'll not tell you of that sadness here, for I
have told elsewhere of my strange meeting with
little Muk-pi and the even stranger ending to
the story of my Eskimo Butterfly. I shall try
to forget to-day the inevitable tragedy of that
story's ending, and remember only its friendly

warm beginning—see Muk-pi as I knew her that
first winter and remember only those ideals of
love and loyalty to her own people which built a
shining wall of refuge for her, even against
hunger and the cold, and made even of months
of silence and the semi-dark a source of strength
and light.

It was because I found her so far away from
home, so lonely amongst strangers, that we came
close together. If I had known her first as I
was to know her later, surrounded by her own
people, I think that she would not have spoken
of her life and theirs with all the intimacy she
used that Fairbanks winter. When we are in a
far country, deserted, hungry, and have lost the
thing we love and hoped to keep, then hearts are
open even to the stranger who shows some bit of
human kindness, and "people-never-seen-be-
fore" become less strange, in primal sisterhood.
In such a setting, we like to talk of home and all
the dearly intimate ways of home. So Muk-pi
opened up her heart to me, "The-tall-white-
woman," and told me of her people in those days
of a long northern winter, while she helped me
sew and knit with her deft busy fingers—
Muk-pi's tiny hands, almost childlike and yet so
tensely strong. And Muk-pi's dainty feet were
so slim and oriental, small, yet they had mushed

down from the farthest north of all our continent,
a trail of frozen rivers deep in winter cold, most
part unblazed and near a thousand miles to
go.

Those talks began and ended with a moon; for
when we'd learned of her predicament and fash-
ioned out a way by which, with the first river
boat when Yukon opened, she was to be sent
back to her own people, she began to count the
moons and would talk of little else.   The word
" January " meant nothing to my Muk-pi.   Why
should it, for what could Muk-pi know of Roman
two-faced god of new-year and beginnings, seeing before (as all of us must do, who see wisely)
by also looking backward?   This was " The-cold-
moon " or " The-moon-when-you-eat-scraps "—
for dark January days are a poor hunting season
for Muk-pi's people.   Or, because one must stay
indoors then, January is " The-moon-of-turn-
ing "—not because the year turns then or the
sun turns back to us North-livers, as I first
thought when Muk-pi told me this, but for a
simpler reason.   It is the time of longest winter
days, when men and boys, in the kashim or com-
munity council house, kill time by spinning tops!
So January was " The-spinning-moon," *wi-wik*
—and there was one month of her waiting spun
away.

" But what comes next, little Muk-pi? "

"What *you* call him, next moon?" Muk-pi
countered. And so I told of Februus, Lycean
Pan, who kept the Roman herdsman's flocks from
wolves.

" All same, wolf catch him reindeer," Muk-pi
nodded, with quick comprehension. " My people
make him, moon, one other name. My people,
in below-country, call him ' Much-moon,' (for
February nights seem long). Other man, my
people, call him *nai-ikh-chik,* Time-first-seals-
are-born. My people no say, all same you say,
' What month is? ' My people say, ' What doing, straight up there? ' And then my people
point him finger, top-side sky. My people know
uk-shuk (a shivery word they have, for winter!)
go now, pretty quick. What name your people
make, *next* moon come, Missis Day-vees? "

Another Roman god! I had forgotten how
much those old gods of war and earth and other
ancient ways had crept into our calendar, so that,
although we live as neighbors to gas engines and
to dynamos, our Temple of Chronos is yet built
in ancient symbols and in antique creeds, upon a
distant and far-gleaming Mediterranean hill.

" You make him, fight, come this moon? "
Muk-pi politely asked, when I told of the War
God. And when I said that Mars' month wasn't

a better fighting time than any other, even
though it might " come in like a lion,"—*then* I
had to explain a lion and had a hard time doing
it, for lions were rather far off Muk-pi's range!
But I painted a polar bear in yellow, gave him
a long swishy tail with a tassel on the end, and
" a big noise." When I tried to make a tropic
jungle for him to live in, however, I was lost—
for jungles were unconscionable, I found, for
tundra-minded folk. I saw that Muk-pi thought
my people very foolish to name a moon for things
that needn't happen in it and animals that lived
so far away—although she made no comment,
but only shrugged a little geisha-like shoulder
and said primly:

" My people call him next moon *ti-gigi-lukh-
chik,* Time-of-the-creeping-on-game. (And I
found later, when her hunter brother Chick-em
told me, that this is the season for seal-stalking,
on the ice.) A more nice name, you may-be
think, people below say (south of the Yukon, did
she mean?) ' Time-of-hawk-come.' My people
some time say, this moon, ' Time-take-hares-in-
net.' You like him, name? My brother, he go
hunt. My brother, Chick-em, he big hunter man.
You see him, you go Nome, Missis Day-vees.
My brother wife, Maw-graw-gee, have plenty fat
bay-bee. He like bay-bee, plenty good. My

brother make—how-you-call little man, for bay-bee?"

"Doll," I suggested.

"'Doll.' Him funny word! My brother make him ' doll ' for bay-bee. With knife he cut, deer-horn, walrus big-tooth, make doll. Maw-graw-gee build him little parka, out from mouse-skin, may-be. Make neck-string (necklace), arm-string, for him doll; cut pretty color bead, may-be. Make little sled, for boy bay-bee. Plenty arrow, all same man. Make foot ball, fill him full, deer hair. Plenty good, kick game! Bay-bee make big laugh, all time play.

"My brother, Tuk-tuk, cut him ivory, good. He make cut, all same white bear. Put some hole, in him; cut hunt-spear. Bay-bee throw, him spear. Stick spear, in hole, him bear. Bay-bee make big laugh. When he grow big, he hunt big white bear, may-be—hit him, *good!* You see? Tuk-tuk make snow knife, ivory, cut much picture on him—picture seal, wolf, whale-with-tooth (narwhal). Bay-bee cut snow, with him knife; make him little igloo. Make man, make white bear in him snow. Hit snow bear, with him hunt spear. Kill him, snow bear, quick! Bay-bee make plenty laugh, *that* time!"

"But what's the next month, Muk-pi—the month when spring begins to come?"

" What you call, ' spring '? "

" When winter, *uk-shuk,* goes—when sun comes home. My people call him ' spring.' "

" My people call him, ' *u-pi-nukh-kuk.*' My people say, good time come, now. More eat. My people say, now, *ningla* (cold weather) go. *Ninglikaqtirutakan taugwam kuttrat tketlaqtut.* There-is-no-more-cold-weather-after-the-coming-of-the-cranes. (April is the time, upon the Yukon Delta and the coast of Bering Sea, when the myriads of geese, ducks, cranes, and other migratory birds begin to come—cranes last, so that their coming always marks the close of Arctic winter.) May-be my people call him, ' Geese-come-time.' My people call him moon, ' Time-to-open-summer-door-to-igloo.' "

" That's strange," I said. " Our name for that month, April, means ' the opener,' too. And the next moon we call May, ' the grower,' because Maia was a star—one of seven lovely sisters—and in old days the people made a feast to her, on May day, because Maia Majesta was the goddess of Spring; and her boy Hermes wore a cap with wings, and could run fast like quick-silver. You know—the weather teller in the ' weather stick.' That is my people's story of the next moon. What do *your* people call him, little Muk-pi? "

"Next moon have good name, 'Time-of-egg,'" she said. "My people go get, plenty. Plenty bird, make plenty egg, *him* moon. My people make one other name, *Kai-akh-tug-o-wik,* 'kyak-going-time.' Plenty animal come now, from below-country—white swan, whale, big salmon. My people work plenty hard, make hunt, make fish, catch plenty bird. Long time, winter come, may-be no eat. Plenty empty dish, in kashim. Hunter work, plenty hard now, all time —have big eat, winter. Old sea-ice break, now. People go all time kyak, hunt. *Ki-uk* come now, plenty soon—what-you-call summer.

"Next moon have fish name. 'Time-of-white-fish,' Down-below-people call him; 'Time-of-sal-mon,' Nome people call him. Long, long ago, *u-ka-mi,* more plenty deer him moon (Caribou fawn in May, so by June there are truly "more plenty" deer!). Now no more wild deer, my people. Long ago plenty wild deer. My people call him moon *No-akh-chug-u-wik,* Time-of-lit-tle-deer-(fawn)-hunting. Now plenty wild deer, your country, no wild deer my country. All go, long time. Chuck-chee deer come, now, my country. (She meant the reindeer brought from Asia.)

"Pretty word, next moon, my people.—You think, Missis Day-vees, come that moon, Big

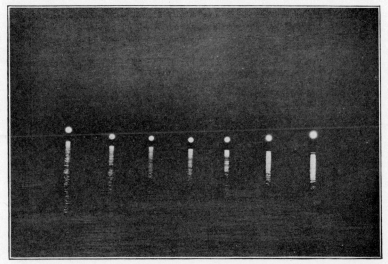

THE ARC INDICATED BY THESE 7 EXPOSURES COVERS AN HOUR AND A HALF AT MIDNIGHT. IT IS 1/16 OF THE VERTICAL CIRCLE OF THE SUN, WHICH IN THE SUMMER HERE SWINGS HIGH IN THE NORTH. THE SKY APPEARS DARK, FROM OVER-EXPOSURE (7 TIMES). IN REALITY IT IS OF COURSE INTENSELY BRILLIANT.

THE REVERSE OF THE PICTURE ABOVE—NOON AT FAIRBANKS AND ONLY A GLOW SHOWING, TO THE SOUTH.

THE TRAPPER BUILDS HIS CACHE ON STILTS, WELL ABOVE THE THIEVING WOLVERINES.

THIS BIG BEAR WAS STARTLED ONCE TOO OFTEN.

River open, good? Muk-pi make go, on boat, all
same you say, may-be? See Chick-em, Tuk-tuk,
plenty brother bay-bee?"

"The Yukon will be open for the boats in
June, Muk-pi, and by July you'll be well on
your way, down-river to your people, on the very
first boat. I've promised that.—What is the
pretty name your people call July?"

But Muk-pi, with her oriental courtesy,
seemed to feel that she had been monopolizing
all the talk, in her heart-turning toward that dear
drear Arctic coast of home, from which she had
been absent in the inner lands and east lands for
five, long, interminable years. Or perhaps she
was just curious about my people's strange
names, as I was about hers.

"How *you* call him, ' Joo-lye?' Him say
' boat-come,' may-be?"

Again a trip to Rome! So I told something
of great Julius and Augustus, chiefs and sha-
mans of my people, mighty men of valor in the
old days—*u-ka-mi,* very-long-ago. But no one
man of all her truly democratic tundra folk was
ever raised so high he had a moon named for him;
and so this seemed a strange and unwise custom
to my little Muk-pi, I could well see, and one that
was but partly comprehended. I tried to tell of
laws they made that still are kept after so many

years; but that meant nothing to a person of
a race that knows and needs no codes. Great
Roman roads could mean still less, for why
should one need roads when there is ice in winter
for a sled and water in the summer for kyak or
umiak? She shook her head.

" Muk-pi no see, so big man, Jool-yus See-zar.
So big man, no can walk good, may-be much
new ice. No savee, how come, Jool-yus See-zar
moon, Au-gus-tus moon. No see him, law.
White man no all same, Innuit."

Innuit is the Eskimos' own name for their own
kin, meaning " the men," " the people." The old
French form of Esquimaux, given by early Jesuit fathers in the east, came from an Indian word
that meant " Raw-meat-eaters "; but no true Eskimo—the shorter Danish spelling used in
Greenland—thinks of himself or calls himself
by any other name than Innuit. So too, does
Tinneh mean " the people," and Thlingit, too.
This seemed a strange thing, when I first came
to Alaska, until I remembered how apt we all
are to consider that *we* are " the people "—of
divine heritance, chosen,—and that our own
tribal habits must be universal laws. When we go
traveling, we too are apt to think all foreign
people " queer "—but thee and me!

After Muk-pi had gone back to her people, I

too made a trip down-river to Nome and up the
coast to where the continents come close together
and one can look across at Asia and out into the
Arctic. Chick-em the hunter told me of his seal-
stalking, Tuk-tuk the ivory worker told me
of The-great-beast-which-lives-under-ground but
dies if it comes up to the air—the pre-historic
mammoth, whose bones are found all over this
part of Alaska. He showed me how he made his
round or oval beads from its long tusks, with
patient cut and polish. He gave me an exquisite
string of fossil-walrus-ivory beads, colored to
rich brown by their long lying in a mineralized
soil and with flicks of deep red and of hunter's
green caught in their dusky shadows. These
were the rarest treasures of all his years of fossil
carving, in which he was so clever; and he said,
with earnest seriousness, that I must have them
because I'd been,—or so he thought—"Long
time, good girl, my sister. You take. I give.
No money. You good girl, long time, my sister."
And so I took the beads, and dearly treasure
them in memory of little Muk-pi.

One day out at the Native village on the Sandspit, where Muk-pi and her sisters were summer
busy making a fine pair of reindeer-leg mukluks
(Native boots) for me—chewing the tough seal
soles to pliability and stitching fancy patterns on

the tops in white- and natural-brown reindeer checkered design—I went back again to that unfinished roll-call of the moons, for I did want to keep a memory of full year with Muk-pi's people. In the meantime I had thought of our own use of the expressions " Harvest Moon " and " Hunter's Moon; " so I could now tell Muk-pi that my people, too, named moons for things that really happened in them! She liked this, I could see, and told her sisters all about it, in that swift cluck and clack of k sounds, so plentiful in all the Eskimo chatter. That my people, too, hunted and harvested, seemed to give me more caste, in their eyes! I had been a little worried lest I couldn't quite explain what " harvest " meant, for I knew the Innuit understood no farming as we know it. But I found these women all smiling understanding.

" My people cut grass, all same your people, Missis Day-vees. My people call him, cut grass, *chan-gut.*" And then she showed me dried seashore grass, of which a pad is put fresh daily in the sole of mukluks as the very best protection against cold feet, in winter. Every morning a fresh wisp is neatly folded and tucked down into the boot's sole, and this not only makes a soft cushion for the foot to rest on, but absorbs all the foot moisture like a woolen sock. It's only one

of that score of clever tricks the Innuit have
thought up, all by themselves, and which so
amaze all those of us who know them: the Arctic
sled and dog harness, which make them winter
kings of Native transportation; the structure-
perfect snow dome of the igloo; the scientific
heat-conserving entrance and wall of their winter
houses; the decked kyak, which is unsurpassed
for one-man water hunts; their waterproof clothing, for rainy days or wet sea travel; the open
umiak or large skin boat, so deftly made, so light,
and holding such amazing tonnage of freight;
their sinew-backed bows, their traps and snares
of infinite variety; the heat-holding one-piece
parka, a perfect garment for cold weather.

Before winter comes, the women of Muk-pi's
people gather quantities of this sea grass, cut,
dry, and store it in a safe place. Mat straw they
call *tup-e-gah-kak*, and they know how to weave
and twist straw, too, as Muk-pi showed me, into
sleeping and sitting mats, baskets, socks, and
very absorbent towels. I had been taught that
Eskimos lived solely upon meat; but I found this
not true, though it is true that meat forms a large
portion of their diet and, where there is no sugar
to be had but plenty of fat, much body fuel of
fat is eaten, sensibly, to keep the body warm in
those long northern winters. Muk-pi showed me

special root-picks which each woman had, with handles of carved bone or painted driftwood— for no trees grow in all her far-stretched tundra land. With these the women go out hunting edible roots, of a certain kind of grass; and these were either eaten raw, when they have a sweetish nutty flavor, or were boiled like chestnuts. The field-mice set great store by these same roots and gather winter caches of them. So Muk-pi and her sisters (wise, as are all her folk in the sly ways of beasties) feel around with a staff for these root-caches, in special known tundra places; and when they find a soft spot, they rob the hard-working field-mouse of his larder! This search is made a jolly picnic time, and is no end of fun. I never saw such good-timey people; and when with them I realized why, and how much, my Muk-pi had been desperately homesick for them and all their social, friendly, cheerful, jest-and-songful ways.

In the spring, young willow leaves are boiled and eaten for "greens," and willow bark and catkins are mixed with tobacco in the long-stemmed, small-bowled, oriental pipes the men smoke. Roots of wild parsnip are roasted in underground ovens, and in the autumn we went after blueberries, heath berries, and salmonberries, while cranberries are stored and used just as we use them, for winter feast-days. Wild sorrel will be gathered, boiled, and crushed with a pestle, then put into a wooden tub as we make sauerkraut, covered with water, and left to ferment in the sun. This has a not unpleasant taste and will be used in winter as a relish with meat, much as we use horseradish.

Muk-pi insisted that I meet every one of her kinsmen, as well as all the visiting King Islanders, Kotzebue Sound, Diomede and even Asiatic Eskimos gathered at the Sandspit for summer trade and visitation. So we had daily rounds of calls, and each tent or up-turned umiak shelter which we entered meant another round of food offered, for her people are extremely openhanded and hospitable. Some of their food was not palatable to me, I'll admit. But Muk-pi had been made deadly sick, at Fairbanks, by eating one of my own very best mince pies; and I've been told Mahatma Gandhi almost died of indigestion the first and only time that he ate beef— the sacred meat, forbidden to his people. You can't account for tastes! Pup seal meat is delicious, though, and blubber (of which we ignorant white people make fun) is used by them just as we use melted butter to dip our steamed clams in, or bits of broiled live lobster—that is, to give meat added flavor.

They're very fond of bone marrow and have made special marrow-spoons to dig it out with— spoons shaped of deer-horn and etched with figures of the family totem, like a crest on our own silver—as well as bone-breakers of white quartz, like nutcrackers. Dippers, spoons and ladles are carved from spruce driftwood which they have steamed and bent, are painted in black and red, are sometimes ivory trimmed and inlaid. I've heard it said that Eskimos are funny people, because they eat fat with a spoon! But so do we, after we've mixed it with some sugar. We call it " hard sauce!" Frozen meat isn't half bad to eat and tastes a lot like very hard ice-cream; while bits of fresh raw meat taste—well, how does a raw oyster taste? Muk-pi and her sisters boiled reindeer, mountain sheep, seal, walrus meat in sea water, and that gave a pleasant salty flavor. And Innuit *do not drink* seal oil, except for the same reason we ourselves drink mineral oil!

The only really impossible food I was offered by Muk-pi's friends, was the one delicacy they found most delightful, I'm sorry to say. I had the same queasy feeling once in Turkey with a confection offered there, and for the same reason, I think—an unusual combination of fat and sweet, unpleasant to the *eye*. *Akutak* is a mix-

ture highly esteemed, and though I couldn't eat
it, Muk-pi told me exactly how it is made. I'll
pass the recipe along, so you may try it if you
wish, though you must first catch your reindeer!

Take a quantity of seal blubber (much like
butter) and a broad slice of the back fat of reindeer (much like bacon). Boil together until the
whole has dissolved. Add a quantity of salmonberries or blueberries. When this has cooled,
stir in vigorously a quantity of hard and very dry
snow. Then whip, until the whole is a stiff
cream.

It looks worse than it sounds, for the blueberries make it a deadly inkish purple-black; and
I am sure it was my eye, and not my nose or
palate, that said " no " so decidedly!

July is " Time-of-braining-salmon," Tuk-tuk
told me, August the " Time-for-breeding-geese-
to-molt." Later with September comes " The-
time-for-young-geese-to-fly " — or " Time-for-
velvet-shedding " a reindeer herder said. October is *Chup-whik,* when mush ice forms, while
others called it *Tin-u-tit,* the flying-away or bird-
migratory moon. But Muk-pi called it " mask-
time," for later in that month is a masquerade
feast, very much like our own Hallowe'en, when
boys and young men go about masked from house
to house and are given presents of berries to put

in the bowls they carry, after which they all go back to the kashim and have a great feast. November is the " Moon-of-remembering-the-dead " (All Souls! I thought, and couldn't help marveling how much our human festivals are of one pattern, embroidered on the seamless coat of Time) and of that other great feast of Harvest-from-the-sea (Thanksgiving!) when the spirits of all sea-beasts caught that year are turned back to their home, with song and festival, that next year's sea-harvest may be plentiful. November is also the " Drum-dance-moon " and " Time-of-muskrats." But December is the " Time-of-feast " moon, real holiday and family-get-together festival.

Then, against the stillness of the ice-closed sea, the lights of the aurora shaking ghostlike across heaven, Muk-pi's people shut out *Uk-shuk* altogether in the warmth of dusk in low oil-lighted kashim and, while the mossy wicks burn high in old carved soapstone lamps, they feast, dance, sing, give one another presents, or repeat in their soft-throated Innuit speech those legends of old days which have been handed down from old men to the young, time out of mind, since the first Raven spirit dwelt alone and made the image of a man in clay, a dog to help him travel, and *tuk-tu* the caribou: stories of wars or " hostile

tidings," children's stories which are the " belong-
ings-of-the-women," stories of " before the time
when we had iron—and when men talked like
dogs; " stories of Sedna, mistress of the under-sea
world; the tale of the woman who married the
Black Bear; of " the-owner-of-the-forest " spirit,
whose children are brown bear and other inland
beasts; of the winds, which are kept by an old
woman living in the North; of Echo, " the-girl-
of-the-mountain voice "; of the Swan-woman,
" pretty as fire "; of the Sun and Moon, who are
brother and sister; of thunder and lightning,
made by two old women who live alone and
quarrel, throw things about, upset and break the
stone lamp on its wooden post; of the shaman,
who had a small gray bird with a blue breast for
his familiar.

And when the old man finishes his tale, he'll
say, "*Nangnok,* it is the end; " or, " I have
spoken many words, and now the wind is dead,
for I have put it out."   Then, pouring a cup of
water on the floor, he'll say:

" Drink well, spirits of all things of whom I've
spoken."

XIII

Sea Bear and Other Arctic Boarders

We tracked our seal to his secret place,
  We heard him scratch below;
We made our mark and we watched beside,
  Out on the edge of the floe.

We raised our lance when he rose to breathe,
  We drove it downward—so!
And we played him thus, and we killed him thus,
  Out on the edge of the floe. . . .

Au jana! Aua! Oha! Haq!
  And the yelping dog-teams go.
And the long whips crack and the men come back—
  Back from the edge of the floe.

KIPLING.

MUK-PI'S hunter brother, Chick-em, often
told me of his meetings with that one of
Nature's great noblemen who is lord of the
Arctic ice—The White One with the royal robe
to whom we have given such high-sounding titles
as Ursus Maritimus or Thalassarctos! But Innuit call his majesty Nanook, and they respect
him above anything that walks the snow.

Nanook wears a nine-foot-long cloak of dense
and oily pure-white fur, which reaches down and

nearly covers even the soles of his feet with such close-set hairs that he can walk securely on the slipperiest ice. He can swim and he can dive, and he prefers a sea-food platter to which he helps himself at his whim from the shelf of his Ice-Floe Cafeteria, in the heavy surf or on the broken ice frequented by the seals. He will eat his fill of walrus, whale carcass, bird eggs, fish, mollusks or sea weeds. A mighty hunter is the Sea Bear, and can make his tremendous sixteen-hundred-pound bulk unbelievably small upon the ice, stretched out flat with neck and black-tip snout laid close against the snow, pushing himself along with patient hunter progress to a seal hole, stopping dead and blending perfectly into the great white silent seascape if a seal but stirs. Only his eyes, nose and pads are black, all else is winter white. No matter how deep cold the outer air may be, *he* can always warm up in the sea! He loves such icy baths, which don't feel one bit icy to him, so deep is that layer of fat under his oily thick fur.

In the spring—" when the Pack wakes and the Old Ice speaks "—the Great White Bear will keep well to the borders of the pack-ice out in Bering Sea and drift with it up into his own ocean that is so well named for him, for Arctic means The Bear. He doesn't like Nome's summer cli-

mate but goes a-sailing both spring and fall; for
when the young ice forms again, the flying-south-
of-birds is over, and October brings the Arctic
ice to close the Bering Straits once more—then
Nanook and many of his royal cousins come riding down out of the North upon the floating ice-
pack, landing preferably at the Bering Sea
islands of St. Lawrence or St. Matthew, where
polar bears soon become too winter numerous for
people's comfort! He much prefers these islands
to the mainland coast, where he is seldom seen;
for he isn't really a land animal at all but a true
Sea Bear, with the sea as his chosen home. A
polar bear, they tell me, is seen only rarely on
the mainland south of Bering Strait, has never
been found as far as twenty miles inland, but has
often been met swimming *in the open sea beyond
landfall!* All he asks is a raft to perch and climb
out on for just a little, like any hardy swimmer,
and the Arctic ice-floes provide him that. Whalers who have timed him say that he can swim
from three to five miles an hour.

"Him smell very good. Him smell dead
whale twenty mile, maybe. Him go up on ice
hill, lift up him head, stick out him nose very
long. Him meat good eat. Him see good. Him
no get snow-blind, all same Innuit. Him look
all-time sun. (His eyes have a membrane like

a bird's eye, I am told, which he can drop down to sheathe them and protect his vision in the glare of ice-fields.) Him no hear good. Him swim with him arm, no with him leg all same white man."

So Chick-em says. Chick-em and Tuk-tuk think white men are strange creatures to want to swim at all! Most Eskimos don't approve of it, any more than do the Tinneh Indians; and I'll admit that usually the temperatures hereabouts aren't conducive to swimming. But the polar bear does swim superbly, and with his legs held straight out behind him. He appears to use them only as steering-gear but he can lunge forward in the water when he wants to, amazingly far and fast. And when, as Chick-em told, he climbs up on an ice hummock, rears up his head, raises his black-tip nose and snuffs the wind—looking out with his far-sighted eyes all over the adjacent open country—he swings his head slowly back and forth on its heavy, long, almost reptilian neck in a peculiar snakish motion like a giant white dragon, wise and old, royally surveying his undisputed kingdom of the icy sea. Yet even in the old days, "before the Innuit knew iron," there were stout-hearted hunters who concealed themselves among the ice hummocks and, as The White One passed or when he had been brought to bay with dogs, killed him with stone-pointed lances, cunningly piercing that *one* spot between the ear and eye, where the great skull is thinnest.

" On shore," Stefansson has written, " polar bears usually try to get away, but on the ice they are royal masters.   They are familiar on the ice with but three living things: seals on which they live, white foxes which they unintentionally provide with food but which never come near enough to be caught themselves (and which are but a mouthful, anyway, about the size of a big cat or a fat Arctic hare, although they seem much larger because of their long and very bushy tail), and the gulls which cry and flutter about them at their meals."   Stefansson is writing of the far Arctic, where His Highness is always attended by a court of white foxes, shadowy flitting ghosts of the Arctic night which follow him like king's jackals and eat the leavings of his royal feasts.

The White One knows but one day, from March to September—but one night, from October to February.   In lush Arctic midsummer he makes love, amid beached floebergs and the short-lived Arctic flowers.   Unlike other bears, only the female hibernates and only in occasional breeding winters, so I am told; but the male will all times roam and range his namesake sea. Eskimos have a tradition that this royal aristocrat takes but one mate. The female dens in snowdrifts tunneled many feet deep and such a den, when dogs will sometimes sniff it out in the late spring, is always remarkably clean, for body and bowels have been winter torpid—the mother bear having stored up so much fat in her tissues that she sustains herself and can provide milk for the cubs, too. Queen Mother almost always comes out in the spring leading two very small and nearly naked cubs, no bigger than Arctic hares. She is a very devoted mother, and Eskimo and hunter lore of the North is full of tales of her intelligent and kindly consideration for these little fellows, which are soon to grow so very big.

I have a beautifully furred polar bear skin under my feet as I write—a skin which has a curious history for it is really the citizenship papers, so to speak, of one of Muk-pi's young cousins. This boy was out on the spring ice hunting with his father, just before the pack was due to move. Now a lad of the Innuit, so they told me, only becomes a full voting member of his tribe when he has killed, all by himself, a walrus, a seal, and a polar bear. This boy had killed the first two and was eager to get his bear before the great Arctic ice-pack moved north and swept the sea of them for that season. Then he saw his father being chased by a huge bear, out over the ice, for father had been caught without his gun; but the boy took after them and killed his bear. While the two men were skinning out the beast, however, their rejoicing was cut swiftly short for the wind had hauled around and now the ice on which they stood was cracked loose from the shore and had begun to move out to sea.   Fortunately, kinsmen who were hunting nearer shore saw what had happened, followed after them in boats, and rescued father, son, bear skin and bear meat from the north-going floe. That great skin, scraped of all fat *just* down to the hair roots and no further, staked down on the snow to dry and bleach, its deep strong fur shaken and brushed until the skin and hair are a pure white, is now my precious rug.

Sir Hubert Wilkins, when in Fairbanks during March of 1926, reminded those of us he talked to there of one thing we'd forgotten, I am sure, if we had ever known it. Antarctic means "opposite of Arctic," of course, but it really is the opposite of Arctic in more ways than merely being located on the other side of the earth! The Arctic is an ocean surrounded by the greatest land masses of our globe, while the Antartic is a continent encompassed by the widest oceans; and the Antarctic has different forms of life, for no people and no polar bears live there. Antarctic could just as well be spelled An-arctic—" without bears." But the North is full of life, and the Arctic hunter finds an almost pure white animal kingdom here—white bears, white foxes, white owls, and sometimes even white moose and white wolves. I have occasionally seen white caribou in Alaska but these are sports or freaks, though white reindeer are sometimes bred.

The Arctic fox, however, has a normal winter coat of white, while its summer pelage is smoky brown as is the summer coat of ermine or weasel. The white fox is so much more common than the blue fox, which is another color phase of the same Alopex, that the white pelt is worth only about a quarter as much. And the Arctic fox is tiny, only about half the size of a fine big red fox. White foxes are now being successfully " ranched " at Teller and at Schismaref on Seward Peninsula; but the Meade, Chipp, Colville and Kaparuk rivers on the Arctic drainage of Alaska, from the sea back to timber line, embrace a wind-swept, untrapped, tundra and barrens area where thousands of white foxes roam in freedom. Arctic foxes will leave the land and go to sea on the ice in winter, where they scavange for Ursus Maritimus and snatch the droppings from his table.

" I doubt'na, whiles, but thou may thieve;
  What then? Poor beastie, thou maun live! "

The King leaves half or three quarters of his
kill. Often he eats only the blubber of a seal
he's caught, and the little foxes, white and
ghostly in the half winter dark, follow him and
take all that he leaves them. Stefansson thinks
the white fox is quite as much of a sea animal as
the polar bear and that probably ninety per cent
of white foxes spend their winters on the ice,
though Innuit hunters tell that some white foxes
lay up stores of dead lemmings and Arctic hares,
and den in winter. They say that " almost any
one, with almost any trap, can catch him," for
Alopex is either too trustful or foolhardy. Like
so many other north-adapted animals, the soles
of their feet are hair-covered, and this has given
them the Greek nickname *lagopus* or rabbit-
footed. Their ears are not sharp-pointed as are
those of other foxes, their muzzles are shorter,
and their fur is dense, very woolly, deep, soft and
pure white, for Alopex lagopus keeps himself
very natty in his snowy coat. There is nothing
to be seen of him but tiny points of black against
the background of an Arctic white—eyes, nose,
and lip, and his dark claws. His cousin, the
aristocratic, fashionable " blue " fox, is raised

successfully on the Alaska Peninsula and the
Aleutian and Pribilof islands, where maltese-
colored coats almost entirely replace the white;
but white coats seem to be the rule wherever there
are either deep snows or hard winters. People
who can't afford the natural " blue " wear scarves
of little Arctic foxes that have been dyed a blue,
steel, taupe or rose to supply the popular trade,
for the fashionable translation of " Lady into
Fox " must continue!

Seals are perhaps the most useful animals of
all the Arctic Sea, though when the man of the
North says " seal " he does not usually mean the
fur-seal of our grandmothers' treasured winter
coats—an animal which migrates yearly to the
Pribilofs in Bering Sea, to breed—but the hair-
or common-seal, which lives here year round.
Chick-em's search for seals under the ice is really
more like prospecting, it seems to me, than like
hunting as we generally think of hunting. He
goes about it very much as a man explores for
oil, and through long centuries of watching, the
Innuit has learned to spear a living out of air-
holes in the ice—*chik-kwelth-kok,* " where no ice
is "! Chick-em knows that seals are seldom if
ever found under *old* ice and are not to be found
where the ice lies in high ridges, but where it is
flat. He knows that seals can find food any-

where in the ocean but *must* come up to breathe, for they are mammals and not fish. Dogs will sometimes discover these breathing holes for hunters, where the seal has pushed his head up through young ice which he can break if it's not more than two or three inches thick. The prospector for seals knows too that open leads in the ice are the accepted routes of travel. With all that he has learned and knows of seals, with all his people's lore, and with his white man's " long eyes " (field glasses), Chick-em goes a-prospecting for seals.

There are three ways of sealing, suitable for early fall, winter or spring. In September the hunters will begin to overhaul their rawhide nets, rig them with floats of inflated bladder and sinkers of stone, bone or ivory, like a salmon gill net. By mid-September the seals begin to come inshore around the rocky headlands and the reefs, and here the nets are stretched, the hunter paddling out each day in his kyak to watch his catch, kill a tangled seal, repair and re-set his net. In deep winter moons, the nets are stretched underneath the ice, grappled and caught from hole to hole, weighted and left floating like a drooping loose-caught curtain there under the hoary-frosted breathing holes, to tangle the unwary seal. Or, on the darkest of mid-winter nights

when there's no moon and even the aurora's
lights are dimmest, the lonely Innuit watcher
builds up his snow wall against the polar wind,
which cuts across this hunched-up shoulder of
the world—and waits and waits and waits beside
a blow-hole for the black velvet seal-cap to rise
through and catch his swift-struck spear-tip.
Sometimes the watcher scratches gently on the
ice with ivory-mounted seal-claws which he always carries, or he whistles low and croons " the
seal song " to tempt the curiosity of this keen-
eared creature.

In spring when leads of water begin to open
once again offshore, or later when the level inshore ice is rotting and wearing into holes, the
seal comes up to sleep and sun upon more solid
cakes. But he does this with caution, and as he
raises up his head from his short seal-naps every
four or five minutes, the hunter must be clever
and very cautious, too. Then Chick-em wears
long white-bear mittens that reach above his
elbows, and creeps prone on the ice, using his left
arm as a shield across his face, dragging his gun
or spear—the bushy white hairs of the mitten, so
similar in color to the dead white ice, serving him
as a blind. And Chick-em showed me, crawling
on the ground beside his house and wearing his
white mittens and white knee-pads, how he could

cleverly steal up upon a seal by playing seal—
crawl slowly forward while his sealship naps, lie
motionless when Mr. Seal looks up, or scratch,
roll, wriggle on the ice like any realistic seal when
the quarry seems to grow suspicious. 'And
Muk-pi's people are such perfect mimics and
born actors that they have learned to " act seal "
to the seal's own taste and unsuspecting doom!

Spring is the great hunting time, when it is
light enough to see well but is still cold; for in
the summer, fresh water from the melt and
streams lies as a layer on top of inshore salt water
and will not support a dead seal, so it is much
more apt to sink when killed and so be lost. Also,
seals are less fat in early summer and this too
accelerates the sinking. So Chick-em likes the
spring hunt best, and often goes a-sealing then.
He will catch his seal as it lies sunning out on
top of the ice, or under it, or in the open water in
between. It makes no difference, except that the
technique of stalking is different. And he must
hunt, for seal is leather for his boots and oil-con-
tainers; it gives him a hundred pounds of meat
and blubber which is food for dogs and men and
a quite necessary body-fuel where sweets are absent in the diet; and seal liver is just as delicious
as calves' liver.

His seal also gives Chick-em light and heat

where wood to burn is lacking; for seal-oil burns
well, though with a black and sticky smudge
which necessarily filled the older Eskimo houses
and made things seem perhaps very dirty. The
seal intestines make his raincoat material for the
wonderful water-proof parka he uses in his kyak.
It is this " rain parka " which makes it possible
for him to turn with the kyak, completely under
water, knowing he'll come up perfectly dry.
They also made fine window panes, translucent
parchment for smoke-hole covers in the older
houses. And Chick-em showed me how you
make a " poke " of a whole seal-skin and use it
as an oil-container, or blow it up and use it as a
float upon a spear-line, or lash several of them
under sleds to make a raft.

Sir Hubert Wilkins told us when he was in
Fairbanks that seals are very plentiful in the
Antarctic, too; and because there they aren't
familiar with either polar bears or human hunters, Antarctic seals are bold and unafraid and so
are easily killed, while Arctic seals are timid, shy,
and very wary through long experience with
skilled Eskimo and White Bear hunters.

Chick-em has his *kam-me-gau-tit* or small flat
drag-sled which he uses when out seal hunting
on sea ice, and onto this he puts his light kyak.
On reaching open water, positions are reversed

and sled goes "top-side kyak"; but when he comes to ice again, off goes boat in a jiffy and on top of sled once more. Long distances offshore are traversed this way, but sometimes wind and current swiftly shift, there is an ominous moment's lull, and then it's time to leave the pack— swiftly, swiftly!—But not always swiftly enough, and then the Innuit hunter must battle alone for perhaps two or three days, to fight his way back to the shore against the moving ice, driven seaward by the winds.

Small wonder that to Muk-pi's people West means "out-to-sea," while East means "in-landwards." And while they have a word which means "very far north," and another meaning "very far south," (for Innuit villages stretch along the coast in both of these directions) they have no word at all for "very far east" or "very far west." They are a tundra people, and neither the dark timberland where hostile spirits lurk, nor open sea with menaces swift as her mercies, can tempt them far from that chosen home-land of The Men of the Elder Ice.

XIV

Meat in Seward's Ice Box

The city was forgot and, parka-skirted,
   We trod that leagueless land that once we knew.
We saw stream past, down valleys glacier-girted,
   The wolf-worn legions of the caribou.
                                          SERVICE.

THE largest piece of meat in Seward's Ice
   Box, as scoffers used derisively to call
Alaska, is the bow-head or polar whale, *ak-bwuk*.
" Toothed " whale or narwhal is also known to
Muk-pi's people, as to the Greenland Eskimo,
and by the same name; while they call the killer
whale " the bad one." White whale too (which
the Russians named Beluga) used to come North
each year in large schools, as soon as there was
open water between the land-floe and the beach.

White whales are only about twelve feet long,
grayish white on flukes and flippers, yellow
tinged along the back. Their blubber is thick,
their flesh good eating, and Muk-pi's people
greatly valued their skin for it made the best of
water-proof soles for boots and also very fine
whale or walrus lines. The hunters took great
pains not to offend the spirit of Beluga, because

227

they wanted him surely to return next year. So every one who helped in killing a white whale, or even helped to take him from the net, must keep quiet and observe a sort of penance or vigil for several days after, while the spirit of the dead whale stayed near its body. No one in all the village was allowed to use a knife or needle, during those days, for they thought these might accidentally hurt the whale spirit still hovering near; and if any parkas or mukluks needed mending during the whaling season, the women had to take them far back on the tundra out of sight and sound of the sea. For all sharp-pointed things offend the whale, and whales are very precious meat.

Old whalers from Nantucket are among my kinsmen, and I know something by report of the trials and arduous dangerous gamble of that greatest of game-taking. To me and mine, *Moby Dick* is one of the world's great epics of a lost race of American heroes. Even to-day, with modern powered boats and the very latest explosive harpoons making small boats unnecessary, whaling is no sport for weaklings, for the Arctic right whale is fifty feet long, weighs many tons, and is thoroughly at home in his sea-haunts. That's why it is the most amazing marvel how Muk-pi's brave ingenious people ever first dared set out in their frail shells of skin to chase and lance this veritable monster of the deep, greatest of dread Sedna's cut-off fingers! How did they ever even dare to dream that they could take him with their puny lance and line,—let alone devise a means which really worked? They lived surrounded on their sea side by these largest mammals in the world, and by sheer nerve and ingenuity made them their meat.

In early May the *omelik* or boat header, a man noted for his experience and success in taking whales, would make up his crews for the whaling season, about ten to a boat. There was great bustle of preparation and umiak covers were renewed and repaired, stout harpoons and lances six or seven feet long were taken out and scraped, seal-skin floats were blown up and fastened then tightly with fine ornamental, good-luck, carved mouth pieces or plugs; and daily the old men of the village met on the shore ice and " talked for an east wind," so that the ice would drive offshore and a lead for whales be opened. For that was how, in the old days, " big meat " came floating into Seward's Ice Box.

But in 1848 an American whaling vessel followed the spring whales north, entered Bering Sea with them, and found their secret summer hiding place. A hundred other vessels followed

up into the Arctic, and from that moment the
meat of Muk-pi's people was in jeopardy. While
the *Plover* was at Point Barrow during the one
year 1853–4, 24 whales were reported taken by
the Natives. When Lieutenant Ray was there
during the two years from '81 to '83, only two
whales were taken by Natives in all that time,
and one of these was just a calf! There you
have the story of what happened. No wonder
that when Sheldon Jackson saw them in 1900, he
found a people half starved and rapidly dying,
through the swift cutting down of their natural
food supplies from the sea—due to the coming of
the whites with guns, explosives, and powered
vessels. Sea game became scarce and wary, and
Muk-pi's people were helpless to compete with
whalers so well equipped.

The Men of the Elder Ice were not quitters.
Food must still be hunted, for if there is no food
one cannot eat, and those who do not eat must
die. Innuit men and women were strong, enduring, knew how to starve as well as how to feast,
and could do both with smiling simple dignity.
They learned to eat but once a day when food was
scarce and to start out at dawn on a long trek
and travel thirty or forty miles, to hunt on an
empty stomach. Early observers said that no
Innuit was known to do a violence to his neighbor

or kinsman, for food; and even when starving, they would not steal from one another, nor eat their dogs, nor resort to that last unthinkable brutality of hungry men. But they were men of the Stone Age, and Iron Age men had come and taken away the meat: a simple thing to us, yet it meant slow death to them. Small wonder that the old men of the people, teaching their boys the patient art of chipping flint, would tell over their work of the happy days before the " white wolves " came to take away the whales and walrus, and when food was always plenty.

The Innuit were very fond of deer-meat, and hides and sinews of wild caribou were in demand and treasured. In old days, herds of caribou such as now roam at will over all of Interior Alaska, had been found also along this coast where Muk-pi's people lived. But whether these particular herds had been destroyed because young Eskimo hunters used to love to chase and capture the young fawns—a test of sport to them, of skill in running and endurance, for even the very young caribou is fleet of foot and runs until his new hooves are worn soft; or whether herds that used to come here changed their route of travel for some new-found better-fancied pastures; or whether, with the coming of Russian firearms to this coast, and later of American whalers and traders, so many more wild deer were wantonly destroyed than men could need for food—I do not know. I only know that once the Eskimo had meat in plenty, of whale and seal and walrus as well as *tun-tu* (deer) and *tun-tu-vak* (big deer, or moose) ; and then, after the coming of the whites, slowly they began to have lean larders, to have to make more dangerous and longer hunting trips, inland and out to sea for game. And though stone lamps no longer lit the kashim with a hazy light but " white-man-light " now lit up brighter cabins, the food-dish was too often upside-down and empty and *muk-tuk* (that choice black whale-skin, which was the meat of feast-day) was something which the growing generation almost never tasted.

Then Sheldon Jackson, education agent for Alaska, visited this sub-arctic ice-fringed sea, the isolated Innuit villages, the huts of driftwood washed upon the beach from Arctic wrecks and Yukon River down-pull. He saw that if these brave people were to be saved from complete extinction, something must be done about it, and at once. He saw that they must be given something surer for a basis of existence than the precarious, then too meagre, products of the sea and chase. Hence, he *did* that something, which was to make this seemingly wild, fantastic and quixotic proposal: that domestic reindeer be fetched outright from one continent to another and Muk-pi's people turn overnight from Stone Age hunters to Iron Age herdsmen! The Reindeer, he claimed—while the whole world hooted at him— would serve as a draft animal, would provide milk and meat, as well as hides for shoes and clothing. "Life would be a different, better thing for the Eskimos, with reindeer as an economic basis," he declared, "in place of seal and walrus and whale."

If Sheldon Jackson had been any ordinary man, the matter would have ended here. But he was not an ordinary man, any more than Father Duncan was; and so the matter did *not* end here! When Congress would not listen, he stumped the country telling how starvation was surely coming to these people of our North—people whose future we had bought when we had made that Russian bargain. He wrote for newspapers, he addressed meetings, he begged subscriptions from kind-hearted individuals. And when he had a couple of thousand dollars in his pocket, he imported—at great trouble—the first sixteen domestic reindeer from Siberia.

When Congress found how well the reindeer throve here—in country that was ideally adapted to their needs, where reindeer-moss covered the land and 300,000 square miles of Alaska's grazing country fairly begged to be made useful—then they made appropriations to help this work, and in all about 1,200 deer were imported in the next ten years and were distributed to Innuit, under a strict apprenticeship system supervised by the Bureau of Education. From this small beginning has grown the present Alaska herd of a million head of reindeer, a new source of food supply for all the U. S. A. and meat once more to fill the shelves of Seward's high Ice Box. Fully half of Alaska's huge area is perfect and million-acred pasture-land for " pasture deer," which the Icelandic word Reindeer means.

Reindeer are merely caribou, tamed; but making tame reindeer out of wild caribou and then herding and using them like cattle, was a trick of man belonging solely to the Old World—until Sheldon Jackson transplanted the first reindeer in Alaska. That is one reason why the experiment was such a tremendous adventure! This one man took a way of life (a culture, reindeer nomadism) well rooted and long familiar on two old continents, and boldly and bodily grafted it upon another people in another and a New World. And it worked! Those sixteen reindeer brought to Teller were a laboratory experiment. The wide industry which has grown out of that experiment, in our workshop of the North, is now a true commercial enterprise.

It would avoid misunderstanding, I think, if people kept the word Reindeer to mean only domestic deer herded by men, such as those animals fetched from Asia—saving the word Caribou for the slightly larger, longer-legged wild animal of the same family, already living here in large numbers. It is just as though we had two separate words for horse, one meaning " tame horse " and the other " wild horse." There's something in the very word Reindeer which implies domestication and there's an equal something in the very word Caribou which implies untamedness, for it came into English through the French, from the old Mic-mac Indian word *Xalibu.*

Climate and the vegetation in the west and north parts of Alaska are very much like those in the Old World where reindeer have been pastured since the first syllable of recorded history. Sheldon Jackson knew that reindeer is the one domestic animal which thoroughly enjoys and really thrives best on a tundra type of pasturage, needs no winter man-made shelter there, and feeds on lichens, moss, mushrooms, grass and willow-sprouts. For ages, domestic reindeer have furnished food and clothes to people living on the northern slopes of Europe and Asia, and now

they're doing this for America, too. Carl Lomen, " Reindeer king of Nome," calls them " The
Camel of the Frozen Desert," and there's a world
of truth in that camel idea! For, like the camel,
it is useful and valuable to the last hair; and like
the camel, too, it lives without care, " off the
country."

Reindeer takes so naturally to tundra because
it has wide hoofs, so that it grazes here without
sinking down in swampy marshy ground, where
sheep or cattle would bog, at once. I always
have to smile when I hear the good old poem
about " The Night Before Christmas " and come
to that line about the " prancing and pawing of
each *little* hoof "! I'm afraid that Clement Clark
Moore was describing eastern woodland deer and
not Santa Claus' true northern ponies; for while
a reindeer is not a very large animal, he is stocky
and his hoofs are quite the most out-of-propor-
tion part of him, being exceptionally large. Dr.
Cantrell says that the tracks of running reindeer
are *ten times* the size of those common deer!

Even more useful than his horns (which both
sexes carry) these hoofs are the most handy tools
the reindeer owns. There is a long stiff bristle
of hair between the split halves of those hoofs, so
that Rangifer (the family name for caribou *and*
reindeer) can keep his footing even on glare ice;

the hoofs are very much concaved and knife-edged like a skate, so that he runs securely on snow or winter lakes and rivers; and there is a small, extra, chisel-shaped bone or auxiliary hoof, dew-claw or clout, just above the quick of each hoof-proper, which gives each foot a four-pointed track and just that much extra support when the halves of his hoof are spread. This is most useful, either in soft mossy tundras or deep snow where moose would flounder on their top-heavy stilts, or as a two-spiked brake when going down steep banks. These clouts touch the ground in running or walking, and give that peculiar clicking crackling sound which is the first thing you will notice about any herd of either caribou or reindeer. The Tinneh say that "Deer hoofs strung up on a line, make winter-music in the shaking wind, like bells."

Their great possible spread of toe is useful as a paddle, when swimming. In the out-stroke, the halves of the hoof are doubled back and contracted, to take up little space; but in the powerful back stroke, they are spread apart and form a wide-bladed paddle. These pointed hoofs are great digging tools, too, and reindeer can remain in the open, the year round, and still find food underneath the snow. There is an automatic oiling system provided for these hoofs, exuding from a gland between the toes; and Lapps claim that the reindeer " oils his horns " with the secretion of this gland, and can " shape his antlers." This is probably said because, when tines of new horns are growing, they itch, and the reindeer gingerly scratches them with his hind hoof— just as you have seen a cow scratch her fly-bitten ear with a careful toe. Sly hunters have discovered that this hoof-oil makes very good gun-grease, if they happen to be " caught out and lack the boughten kind."

Reindeer antlers, too, are large in proportion to body-size—larger than most people realize; for many Christmas card pictures, supposed to be of reindeer, are really drawn from elk. Rangifer's antlers are shed each year, but grow again fully by fall. His call is a peculiar grunt or bark, sounding like *uhrr* said very gutturally —as though some one had poked you suddenly, below the belt! In size, a reindeer is just about halfway between cattle and sheep, the average of dressed reindeer meat shipped from Alaska now running about 150 pounds per animal, though a large wild woodland-caribou bull may dress 300 pounds. So the experts in herding are now cross-breeding wild caribou with tame reindeer, to make our Alaska herds stockier and more beefy.

Like horses, reindeer shed their hair rapidly as warm weather approaches and the color of the short, new, smooth coat is a dark and glossy clove-brown, almost the shade of northern mink. But as winter comes on again, the hair gradually lengthens and becomes a lighter more grayish color. Close compact hair and light-weight skin combine to make this hide ideal for arctic garments, and Eskimos pay fancy prices for white or spotted reindeer that look like piebald ponies, for these make very fancy parkas or muk-luk tops. Lapp and Siberian reindeer herders have specially selected and bred these white and pinto animals because, though not as sturdy as the darker reindeer, their color is so very pleasing. Also, they claim that a few white animals scattered through the herd will make good markers, as black sheep do in a band of white. But no reindeer or caribou is all one solid color, for the under-throat hair is always lighter, long and tufted, hanging in a pendant mane.

Reindeer hair is peculiarly hollow, each hair a little quill full of air, hence very buoyant. It makes fine stuffing for Eskimo footballs, a favorite game with them that's played by men, women and children. This buoyant coat, together with that splendid paddle foot, makes Rangifer the most at home in water of all the

deer clan. When frightened, they will often take
to water—instinctively, I think, for wolves are
the old foe. They will plunge down bank into a
river, the thin spring cows shoving the little
fawns in for their first swim, helping them breast
the current by pushing with their bodies. And
how they swim! I've heard that two men, paddling in a canoe as hard as they can paddle, can
just overtake a frightened swimming caribou.
These little fawns have the most lovely coats,
curly and beaver-colored when new-born, silky
and soft. A parka made of four or five such
skins is breath-takingly beautiful, but it's when
these little fellows are curly soft and small, only
a few days old, they are such easy prey for eagles,
wolves, wolverines and bears. On one trip in the
North, following a caribou migration, we saw
the remains of six to ten calves every day, which
beasts had caught. Yet they say there are three
million wild caribou still left upon the Arctic
slopes.

Thcsc are the least shy of all deer, the most
inquisitive; and while they do not trust their eyes
very much, they do trust their noses! Their foes
are four: wolves, which relentlessly hang on the
fringes of the herd and which alone can run them
down in winter; forest fires, which are the bane
of all timber creatures (and some wild caribou

Photograph by Cann.

"JACK FROST IS IN HIS WORKSHOP OF THE HIGH NORTH."

Photograph by Merrill, Sitka.

SITKA AS IT APPEARS TODAY, THE GREEN CARROT-SHAPED SPIRE OF THE OLD RUSSIAN CHURCH
TO THE RIGHT OF THE NEW WIRELESS TOWERS.

are woodland); a freeze after a sudden thaw, which forms a hard crust over winter snows; and summer insects, especially the bot or warble fly. These pests have given Rangifer the habit of always feeding *into* the wind, and they will seek the windswept ridges and low mountains in the summer, trying to escape this summer bane of any spongy mossland. Lapp herders always say: "Mosquito helps us round the herd up, at spring marking time!"

Reindeer are herded much as sheep and cattle, for they are something like both, and the Eskimo herder handles deer as though he were a combination of western sheepherder and cow-puncher. He lives with his herd and moves about with it, like a sheepherder; he walks with them on foot like a sheepherder (with his dogs, which are sometimes collie crossed with malemute) and doesn't use a horse at all. But he handles a rope and uses a branding corral like a thoroughgoing cowboy, though on foot; and, also like a good cow-puncher, he will disturb his herd just as little as possible. For, as the wise old Lapps say: "The pasture deer is a half-wild creature, still, and he increases best when we don't bother him too much." In winter, the herder will use snow-shoes and ski, to give *him* extra hoofs! Reindeer flock like sheep, and are like sheep in following a leader, as well as in their habit of running single file; but in most grazing habits they are more like cattle and in activity and quickness they are a lot like western horses—less shrewdly intelligent than range horses, but more so than cattle. Although so wide of antler, in general they are gentle-mannered and it's quite safe to walk about in a packed corral, for they are trustful and friendly with their herders. Now that barley is being raised successfully in Interior Alaska, and is being used as a fattener for deer, this feeding proves to be another bond between the herder and his herd, just as corral-fed cattle become very tame.

Although the very name of Reindeer means " flock-beast " or " pasture deer," that pasture must be wide and open, for he carries a gipsy heart under his gray-brown coat; and Dasher and Dancer, Prancer and Vixen, when they wish to travel, generally *do* travel, and herdsmen must follow! Although long a domestic animal, in one sense, it can't even yet be said that reindeer are fully under the control of man. They still have that haunting gipsy streak and all who live with reindeer constantly, as do the Lapps and the Siberian Tungus tribes, must be prepared to be upon the move. That's why both Lapps and Tungus have reindeer schools—teachers who travel about with the herds, real peripatetic moderns.

Sometimes I think that Reindeer controls and shapes the life of Man and stamps his nomad pattern on him, even more than Man shapes and controls the Reindeer life-ways; for, once you take up herding, you must live constantly with and by your herd. Sheep and cattle have had this primitive wanderlust pretty well trained out of them or have sworn off from wandering, as a bad habit, in return for the free board and lodging which Man has furnished. But no man beds down Rangifer of nights, fetches him water in a pail, or fills his manger full of warm bran mash; so he has never come to be as wholly tame as cows and horses. Reindeer still spends his nights under the stars, like his wild congener, and finds Man useful to him mainly in warding off those wolves so constantly making inroads upon the Rangifer legions. So Reindeer remains a very independent creature, restless at times and feeling that same ancient migratory urge he shares in common with his wild caribou cousins.

In Europe, many reindeer herds winter in Sweden and summer in Norway by the seashore, where winds will drive away pestiferous mosquitoes; but, as the Lapp herder sings in his herd-song: " When nights grow darker by the Ocean,

then reindeer yearn for shelter of the forest."
And not only will they swim wide rivers boldly to
reach those forests, as we have often seen the
caribou do upon the Yukon, but are so clever at
it that (in Norway, where they must swim wide
estuaries on their trek) Lapp herders tell me that
the deer will wait until the tide is just on turn—
" When the Sea is full," they call it—and then
plunge in. The Lomens, who have handled deer
for years and own the largest of Alaska herds,
will tell you that the reindeer " know their pasture and their range, their home and, like a hom-
ing pigeon, while they don't fly they surely trek
back to their own home range, when moved from
there—unless restrained by watchful herding or
until they have become thoroughly familiar with
the new environment." And day and night in
fawning season they must be closely guarded,
when the little fellows appear—all legs at first,
for all the world like calves. Then's when your
herder has to be most watchful.

Good reindeer tending requires many of the
very same powers and much of the same imagina-
tion and knowledge which hunters use, and the
sons of Chick-em and Tuk-tuk are heirs to countless, skilled, hunter generations. So they have
taken to their reindeer apprenticeship, like ducks
to water; and in far fewer years than turned

Plains Indians into Pony Indians, Muk-pi's people have caught the trick—quick learners that they are—of this new game. For, though it's only a short time since the first reindeer came to Alaska, people with such observant minds, such intimate familiarity with animal habits and with all the moods of their home tundra-land, have quickly seen that reindeer meant full food-bowls, fat rosy " bay-bees " carried in the parka-hood, and winters full of cheer, not gaunt with hunger. Endurance, quickness, skill in living off the country are Innuit traits *par excellence,* are hunter's traits, are herder qualities, too. So Muk-pi's nephews have grown up to be good reindeer herders, and sometimes even go aloft in planes, to-day, to sweep the range for likely pasturage or look for bunches of lost deer.

In parts of Asia and in Europe, too, reindeer are used for driving; and sometimes they are used so in Alaska. A span of deer can make ten miles in less than half an hour. In Siberia, men sometimes ride reindeer-back, sitting way up on their shoulders where the deer are strongest but not upon the middle of the back, as with horses, though I have never seen this done in Alaska. Away from towns and dog-teams, reindeer make good pack animals, easily trained and, what is more, you never have to worry about supper for them as you do with dogs, for supper is always just underfoot in the moss. But dogs are better for any journey that is more than a week long, because constant work on nothing more than moss proves as trying to a reindeer as constant work on hay alone does to a horse. Besides, the Eskimos are such experienced dog handlers that they don't feel any great need for another sled animal, but use their reindeer mostly as we use our cattle—for meat and hides.

Reindeer steak tastes something like dark meat of turkey, some people think. Many of the best hotels in the States now serve Alaska reindeer meat and it's considered much finer than venison, for it hasn't any gamy flavor but just a slight tang which most people find very pleasant. Some describe the taste as " halfway between lamb and duck." Our government's Bureau of Home Economics has published a pamphlet of Reindeer Recipes, so if you'd like to taste Alaska reindeer, this will tell you the best ways to cook it. And many city markets now sell " sleigh-bell steaks," as I once saw them advertised!

There's meat once more in Seward's Ice Box, so much that Muk-pi's people can now afford to let the rest of us share tastes of it. There is a new wide pasture staked, here in the North, for pasture deer. And Saint Nicholas, patron saint

of that old Russia whose past Alaska shares,
rides high in his High North under the sign of
Ursa Major, driving his fat and antlered ponies
and showering gifts of happier days, through
all the moons, for Muk-pi's people.

XV.

The Frost King's Palace

Day after day was dark as death, but ever and ever at
    nights,
With a brilliancy that grew and grew, blazed up the
    Northern Lights.
They rolled around with a soundless sound like softly
    bruisèd silk;
They poured into the bowl of the sky with the gentle
    flow of milk.
In eager pulsing violet their wheeling chariots came,
Or they poised above the Polar rim like a coronal of
    flame.
From depths of darkness fathomless their lancing rays
    were hurled,
Like the all-combining searchlights of the navies of the
    world.

SERVICE.

IF you live under the Great and Little Bear,
the constellations are your close neighbors;
for the star-litten sky of brilliant winter draws
near and crystal clear when seen through the
un-city-smoke-dimmed medium of an Arctic atmosphere.

Jack Frost is in his workshop of the High
North and aurora borealis, sun-dogs and other

248

mysteries of northern night and day are just a
part of that unreal confronting which makes of
Arctic winter an experience unforgettable to any
mystic-minded person. Less noticeable further
south than at my home town of Fairbanks, more
noticeable further north, in all Alaska we are
subject to the influence of meteorological phenomena, whether we admit it or not. Even the
God of the Golden Bow and of the Golden Lyre,
Charioteer of the patient year—the Sun about
whose movements we have built our calendar—
appears to do strange antics, here. In Arctic
winters, he of the golden hair and golden fire,
from whom we humans have obtained our energy,
directly or indirectly, becomes a sun seemingly
unaware of life or living, so far away he draws
into the empyrean and far cosmic space, and
paints the winter snow a color colder than winter
snow itself. Yet even the extreme cold has a
splendor that is truly glorious. There is a tingle
in your veins, a challenge to your vitality, at forty
or sixty below that is one of the most invigorating
experiences imaginable.

Mild frost-bite is no worse than bad sunburn,
and I've known both. Both merely make the
skin tender for a long time after. I shall not soon
forget that winter solstice trip I made once to
Nenána before the railroad came. When facing

wind upon the river, where the bluffs made fun-
nels, I foolishly covered my face with a scarf, up
to the eyes. The moisture from my breath con-
gealed and froze there in two points on my cheeks
which still are tender. But neither shall I soon
forget the sun that rose a little way above the
southern hills that morning, about half past
eleven. Then as we slowly mushed the dogs
across a wide plain, now softly snow-pastured
but through which the tall gray grasses pushed
their heads, the low and ruddy sun just rising
caught in a swiftly magic flash the hoar frost
thick upon the grass tips and struck in quintaled
crystals their glorified dead leaves and frozen
seed pods. It flung a veritable Sinbad valley of
diamonds, emeralds and rubies before us and
across the open land, touched with blue slender
shadows and with countless threads of mauve
wherever short and level sun threw those long
shadowed grass-stems across the snow fields. In
all the picture galleries of the world I've never
seen a thing that caught my heart so, with
strange beauty.

In the utter quiet of windless winter days I've
realized, as no other where, a sense of the globe's
self swimming through space. Perhaps, too, the
apparent imminent closeness of the moon and
stars in winter adds to that feeling of mighty

movement in swift heavens fleeing past, which makes one actually seem to feel old Earth rolling in her planetary wheel upon her silent axletree. Here the majestic spin of the earth eastward is almost a palpable movement.

In winter when " the northin wind hath purifyit the air " and the sun turns cold and far away, then we confront the shows of day and night, and seem less real than they are. Then, in the duskiness and still, the moon, the moving shadow of the sun, the moving constellations " that still sojourn yet still move onward," creep very close through the quiet fields of vast illuminated space. Then, in early afternoon, we pay our calls by moonlight, for high-riding Diana is circling the heavens without sinking below Earth's rim—unwearying witchly substitute for Sun. In seeming endless benedicite, this lesser of God's candles is alight for us, and dwellers in the North know the long glories of the winter moon—where, Muk-pi's people say, a mighty shaman lives. I had looked forward with some dread to the long dark winters of the North, of which I'd heard such tales—only to find a vast unearthly brilliance here, not darkness; for the winter days are usually not dark at all, in any sense of being a thick night. Even though the chilled sun may not be visible more than an hour, there follows a long and colorful wondrous twilight, and after that the atmosphere is agleam with intense and dazzling moonlight—for long days at a time each month, when in and near the full. For the mid-winter moon at full rides above the horizon by quite as much as the mid-winter sun lingers below; and in the further Arctic it does not set at all these times, I'm told, but circles heaven like our summer sun. Even in sub-arctic Fairbanks, we had " long moons " in November, December and January—white, bright, full glory on the unbroken candent snow from early afternoon till late next midday's laggard sun-dawn.

The large white stars are diamond bright—so much so that I have read by starlight, coming home from winter post-office. Never have I seen such closely burning stars, so clear one notes the differences of color in them, more often read about than noted but actually perceptible here. Muk-pi calls the Milky Way the Snowshoe track of the great Raven Spirit; and winter stars are not to us those " eyes of wolves " of Hiawatha story. The long and dreary winter, the cold and cruel winter, may have seemed very real to a New England Longfellow, but not to us of the actual North. We love the stars, so much so that we miss them dreadfully in the too-long summers, when all the constellations are extinguished and

we don't see any stars for months. We welcome
back again those nights that sparkle with true
northern vigor and clarity. I've never known
an autumn in the North when, some fine day at
evensong, a friend has not called up excitedly by
telephone and cried, " Come out and see the stars!
They're back again!"

And there, in the clean clear-aired sky, one
finds it hung—that first, supreme, forsaken star.
I wish that northern tourists could see our land,
winter caught and lovely in beauty blent with
strangeness, which is the essence of all things
truly romantic. For then, too, these great spaces,
mauve and blue and rose by phantom day, star-
shot by night, unbroken and unperturbed, are
sometimes incredibly alight with the crackling
flame of Aurora Borealis burning like some weird
vasty signal torch from a lost spirit land.

There is bewitchment in Borealis that is haunting, memorable, as marvelous to wondering scientist as to equally wondering savage. Seen
sometimes further south, but seldom seen there
in a maximum display, these phantom quivering
lights of other-worldly green or livid yellow,
sometimes—especially when the weather is
changing and a sudden drop in temperature is
to be expected—will turn from flickering rays of
rose or elfin violet dimly seen, to rise in great

waves of brightness that occupy the constellations
of the zenith and crack across the late autumnal
sky like a great drover's whip, crossing all heaven
with a shot of flame, to flash and flare and die
again. One's hair bristles, one's scalp tingles,
standing in frosty air to witness it. Sometimes
these flaming snaky ribbons seem to sweep so low,
instinctively you wince and side-step, even although you may have read that scientific " trian-
gulation " places the height of the aurora at from
50 to 400 miles above the surface of the earth!
Is it subconscious primitive fear which raises
goose-flesh as you look—a certain chill volup-
tuousness aquiver in you? Or is it the stupendous air-filling electric discharge, which prickles
at your skin in a distinctly felt sensation? I do
not know. It may be both or neither; but this
sense is very real, of that I'm certain, when

> " The light of hell-fire flows
> Into the bowl of the midnight sky—
> Violet, amber and rose."

I've read a dozen fine scientific descriptions of
the " why " of Northern Lights, and I know
less of their cause than I did before! I'm told
that further research into the faery lights of the
Aurora Borealis may well lead to a better understanding of the mysteries of radio, and link it

with that rush of strange electric flame which
makes close-felt aurora seem the whorling symbol
of another world, high, windless, strange. As
yet, they remain a mystery and the Heavens still
a " work of Thy fingers." I suspect that scientists themselves don't understand it, although
polar explorers are to-day hard at work upon the
many problems of this great magnet—Earth.

Another heavenly mystery of frost is found in
those pale mock suns called " sun-dogs," for cold
and frost are a great artist team in lighting effects and accomplish magic which no others can.
Frost crystals clinging in the air are practically
the same shape as the lovely hexagonal prisms
made to beautify great dripping chandeliers in
old ballrooms, and Jack Frost hangs them in the
North for us in a festoon. The low winter sun
shines through and—presto!—we have sun-dogs,
an ugly name to call such weird beauty, but Alaskans talk a dog language! " Parhelion " is pret-
tier, but few Alaskans ever use that Greek-ish
word which means, of course, " beside the sun."
A luminous circle surrounds the sun or moon at
times, formed by reflection and refraction of
light by ice crystals suspended in the atmosphere
—an optical phenomenon as is the rainbow, unreal but no less lovely and far more rare. This
frost refraction makes halos appear at definite

distances from the sun, colored red on the inside
and with just a trace of outer blue or green. The
most brilliant mock images of sun occur where a
raised, white, luminous horizon line appears to
cut the inner halo, the parhelic outer circle (as
of an outer rainbow) being far less brilliant.
Similar moon phenomena are " paraselenæ,"
" sullen nights by moon-dogs haunted."

Parhelia are most intense in color when the
sun, as in our winter noonday, rests near the horizon. As the sun rises, the " sun-dogs " seem to
pass a little beyond the halo and grow flaming
tails. This Danaän fruitage of a shower of suns
to startle and delight our short crisp glimpse of
day, seems beautiful to me, though Service
thought it cruel: " There where the sullen sun-
dogs glare in the snow-bright bitter moon."   I
believe that many, whose permanent dwelling is
the North, feel rather that The Frost King's
Palace has been beautifully decorated as our own
special home, with the great chandelier of sun
hung here at noon, with extra rosy-tinted frosty
bulbs turned on, to make us see that even Frost
and Snow may bless and glorify, forever.

The welcome silence of the snows cannot come
too soon for us, once winter really sets in. In the
low sun, snow is not white but exquisitely tinted
—blue and purple deep in shadow, rose in the

light or violet in the shade, ghost pearl of white under the moon. Only the direct *down* light of late spring brings pure white glare on snow here, for the level, low, refracted light of winter is multi-color of pastel. Snow comes only in relatively warm weather, while in the " deep cold " the air is brilliantly quiet and that's the time " the silences are spawned." Snow is a condensation of moisture, and time and again a news item in our local paper will read, " warm weather brings snow to the Interior." The lower the temperature, the less water vapor the air can hold. The air at zero holds but a tenth as much water as the air on a hot summer day, and very cold air will hold only a very little moisture. Deep cold is dry cold!

Like most difficulties seen from afar, Northern winters when actually experienced prove not difficult at all. Life is organized here for winter and when I first came North I was so busy getting first impressions, making new friends, and learning new ways, the winter was over before I fairly knew it. The amateur may dread it, as the amateur sailor dreads the wind. Later, as one gains skill, technique, assurance, one comes to know the winter cold as the salutary and necessary medium for Northern life. When the earth begins to contract with frost and frost gathers on the upturned collar of your coat, you pay a little more attention to the furnace but that is about all the change it makes in living. The chicken houses must be lighted as well as heated, now, if one would have fresh eggs, and kerosene becomes thick and cloudy at minus sixty. But our houses are so well built, we wear exactly the same clothes indoors that we did in Colorado or New York, and outdoors the same as in Minnesota or the Dakotas.

Fur coats are usual about town, but not absolutely necessary. We don't wear leather-soled shoes on the street but felt-soled shoes, both because cold travels along the shoe nails and because footage in the dry snow, like sand, is less slippery with felt than leather. When you go on the streets in the deep cold, forty below or lower, the air is sharp like glass and fairly crackles. Your breath comes audibly and hangs a little frost-cloud before your face, gathering on your fur collar; and the horses have bigger clouds of frost in front of their noses, which are swathed in burlap to " keep their lungs from freezing." Every one is hurrying, not because of cold but because you feel your blood coursing through your body, and its good speed warms and stimulates you. The invisible frost sings thinly, crisply, in the two-bladed air.

The greatest danger in our winter-gripped town is not from cold but fire, especially in the fall before snow comes to protect our shingle roofs. The Frost King does us little harm, but much of mercy; but when the Fire Slave we have caught and shut to do our work, breaks from his iron box and ravishes, then truly we know panic. The frame and log houses burn like tinder in the crisp air, hose lines are hard to keep unfrozen, and twice our winter town has been swept by fire before it could be stopped. Frost helps even here, however. In the one big fire I've seen, large sheets of canvas were brought out and hung upon the roof and walls of the bank, which lay in the track of the flames. Then fire hose played upon and wetted these tarpaulins and almost instantly they coated in a sheet of rigid ice film, completely protecting the building. We all helped to fight the fire, of course, and I'll not soon forget the sight of Jim Fairborn playing his fire hose on a building which was a wall of ice outside, a flaming cauldron inside! Then, as we watched, he began to stagger. I ran to offer help, thinking him exhausted.

"No—no! My coat," he said, "an axe—a coat!"

I was stupid and couldn't understand; but another did, and ran and fetched an axe and a fur

coat. The spray blowing back from the nozzle
had frozen in rattling ice all over the heavy coonskin coat Jim Fairborn wore, so that the front
of it weighed many pounds and he could scarcely
stand erect under its weight. He had to be
chopped from it, and he clanked like a knight
in armor! He often laughs to-day about the time
when he was " glaciered."

This use of the word " glacier " is peculiar, I
think, to Alaskans, and close to the older French
meaning. We say that a stream has glaciered if
it has frozen over; or when water flowing across
a road freezes, we say the road has glaciered; or
a frozen water pipe or drain is called glaciered.
A real glacier is, of course, " permanent ice on
land," and the largest real glaciers in the world
are to be found in Alaska, unless some new and
larger glaciers should be discovered at the South
Pole.

A true glacier is a mass of compacted ice origi-
nating in a snow field, and glaciers are not peculiar to the North any more than are snow fields.
There are over a thousand in Switzerland, seventeen of them covering as much as six square miles
each. " The Great Aletsch " in Bernese Oberland
is sixteen and a half miles long, but the Menden-
hall in Alaska is twenty-five miles long, and Muir
Glacier has a three-mile front and its " snout,"

resting its tongue on gray-green jadeite water, is
four hundred feet high! Twenty *tributaries* of
the Muir Glacier are larger than the famous
Mer de Glace of Europe; John Muir called the
Stikine Valley " a Yosemite one hundred miles
long," and three hundred glaciers drain into it;
while Malaspina Glacier, flowing down from
Mount Saint Elias, contains fifteen hundred
square miles (one-tenth the total area of Switzerland and larger than the whole state of Rhode
Island) with a sea-front of ice extending nearly
a hundred miles along the Gulf of Alaska.

What is a glacier—and why? It is the child
of altitude and snow perpetual, and that is why
Alaska's glaciers are mostly to be found on the
giant slopes of the South Coast, where Kuro
Shiwo drips perpetually upon tremendous mountains rising abruptly from the sea. Glaciers are
not peculiar to the North, but may be found on
any portion of the earth's surface, even at the
equator, that rises above the permanent snow
line. Here the temperature is below freezing,
evaporation is slight, and so enormous fields tend
to pile up—the snows of yesteryear, or *firn,* being
covered by those of the next, and so on in perpe-
tuity. " If these piles of snow were rigid and
immovable," scientists say, " they would then increase indefinitely in height. All high mountain

regions would be buried in domes of snow, miles in thickness."

When snow has fallen to a sufficient weight, however, something happens; and that something is a glacier! The great mass yields to its own pressure and begins to flow both downward and outward. Thus a balance is established, weight and height are both relieved and the snow field disintegrates at its edges through the flowing out of glaciers, which are the device by which old earth keeps on her steady keel. Otherwise, her rigging and high spars would get all top-heavy with frost, and there might be serious consequences, even capsizing! For,

> " This earth is not the steadfast place
> We landsmen build upon,
> From deep to deep she varies pace
> And while she comes, is gone."

Snow fields become ice rivers, because after each snowfall there is a period of rest during which the old snow becomes compact and granular, undergoing consolidation. This old snow is called *firn* or *névé* and is coarsely crystalline. As loosely-fallen light *neige* becomes in time tight granular *névé,* it slowly turns through pressure into dense clear ice, retaining however its crystalline texture. Long tongues of this compacted ice are pushed out from under the great over-packed mass and move slowly down the valleys—to melt in streams or to crack off whenever they reach the sea, for icebergs are the broken ends of glaciers. This Alpine type of glacier, such as we know in Alaska, is a tongue of ice dropping down a mountain slope—a brittle mass crevassed by any abrupt change of gradient.

The greater part of Greenland is covered by a continental ice cap of another type, 400,000 square miles of ice-sheet a mile thick (for Greenland's mountains really are icy!); and the Antarctic ice blanket is believed to be quite as large as the entire United States. If glaciers from these polar masses did not push out from home and seek to see the world, then the earth would surely become topheavy at the poles and—who knows?—perhaps it might "swap ends on us!" Glaciers keep the old earth spinning steadily, so glaciers are really a great invention. The "glacial period" is a continuing presence in some sections and not a past event, though now the total ice upon the earth is only half as widely spread as during the climax of the Pleistocene, and is mostly confined to Greenland and Antarctica. But we still live in a great Ice Age, with a large fraction of the total land surface so covered.

It is believed to-day that Earth's climate is

born at Earth's poles, and that is one of many reasons why our scientists and explorers have laughed at death and risked the literal ends of the earth to hunt out the Home of the Winds, the Cradle of the Currents, and read the secrets carved upon the Paleocrystic Ice. *Crescat scientia, vita excolatur,* is their cry. Let knowledge grow, life be enriched! If we know the polar areas better, study the movements of Arctic waters, develop the infant sciences of oceanography and earth magnetism, then one day we may be able to predict—perhaps even control—the weather. Who knows?

Earth's Poles have always called and have sometimes shown both wonders and bounty. "The icy blade hid in the white mantle" has not deterred but rather lured adventurers for gain. Adventurers for truth have met that lure and sought to answer in the terms of Science that mocking challenge spoken once to Job:

"Hast thou entered into the treasures of the snows? Where is the way where light dwelleth? As for darkness, where is the place thereof? Out of whose womb came the ice? And the hoary frost of Heaven, who hath gendered it?"

XVI

Forest and River Traps

Unto them in the Long, Long Night came the man-
who-had-no-name;
Bearing his prize of a black fox pelt, out of the Wild
he came.

" Did you ever see such a skin? " quoth he; " There's
nought in the world so fine—
Such fullness of fur as black as the night—such
lustre, such size, such shine? "

SERVICE.

AFTER the October slush ice in big " pans "
has ceased to run upon the Yukon and
November has made solid all the waters, when the
trees of our inner Alaska land begin to crackle
with the deepening cold of Winter and the black
thin-drawn shapes of willows along the great
river courses become fine shadowy lines in the
short dusk of darkening winter days, then the
hunter gets out his gear and the trapper begins
to set his lines. For they have read that ancient
picture-writing in the snow, and amongst the
black-etched winter trees, the frozen hummocks
of the goose-grass in the sloughs, have seen the

265

mark of fox, lynx, marten, rabbit, moose and caribou.

Fannie Quigley is writing me from Kantishna: " I got one cross fox, one mink, three lynx and eighteen ermines, and sold them for $489. We had a good garden last summer and Joe's tunnel is full of vegetables. We went for a hunt and got four caribou, one moose, one bear, and Joe got two mountain sheep on Wickersham Dome. I wish that you could have some! They are good and fat." Muk-pi's people, too, begin to hunt and trap with the first heavy frost and keep it up until the short cold days of deep mid-winter. Then they make indoor holiday until February, when trapping is again taken up until the April sun makes fur too hard and light and brittle to be of any value.

The Innuit are energetic trappers and energetic traders. When the Russians came to the mouth of the Yukon, they made a red fox skin the unit of value, and the old word for one dollar is still " one skin," and fifty cents is " half-a-skin!" It's actual truth to say that all these Native peoples of the North lived in an animal world, for the whole earth was thought of as a humanized thing, in person and in form. We, too, have deified the earth at times. Northmen have made a music out of Erda, " the endless

world's all-wise one; " and pre-Homeric poets
sang of Gæa, "first-born to spring from Chaos,
Mother of Titans." But every part of Earth's
body seems a living substance to our Natives
here, potent with quickening life-power, and all
who feed upon her are alike her children and alike
immortal. Each lake and stream, each forest and
each mountain has its spirit—*inua* the Innuit call
them, the " Things-which-own-the-places "—and
all the world of animals know, so they think, the
same customs and the same occupations as the
world of men. For in what other way could they
think of them?

To Muk-pi, the Beaver was a clever fellow,
able to read men's minds; the little *sik-sik* ground
squirrel was a small young woman, with long
fingers and a handsome gray parka, who
" pounds the roots and makes her cakes of
them; " and the Fox Man was a sly devil, who
wore black boots and a long red coat. For centuries they had been pitting human against animal cunning, in the old lifelong game of hunt
and trap; and Muk-pi's people felt that beasts
were somehow cousins of their own. By all of
our Alaska Natives, the much-sought magic shaman power was thought to be a thing caught
from the animals. To know their ways, to use
their flesh and fur yet not offend their mystic

magic *inua*—those guardian spirits of the animal
haunts, which could withhold or·grant successful
hunt and trap—*that* was their constant study,
their legend, their science, their religion.

And the first Russian comers, the Hudson Bay
and " Boston men," were all preoccupied with
problems of the fur trade, too. Your trapper is
always your original trail blazer, in northern
lands. The fur quest is not only an age-old lure,
but in North America the trapper and fur trader
have been the men who pierce the hinterland, en-
large the colonies, push back the boundaries of
little coastal settlements, and provide those solid
geographic facts upon which later empire builders lay their firm foundations. North America
was a fur-bearing continent, and still is. John
Jacob Astor founded his Astoria, at the mouth of
the Columbia, as an 1811 fur-post. It was seized
and occupied by British in 1813, and its return
after that war gave our young Uncle Sam one
of his strongest claims to the great Oregon Tract,
the whole drainage of the Columbia River; so,
out of fur was built the firm basis, not only of
the largest personal fortune acquired in America
up to that time but also of America's own western boundary. We have the picture John Cor-
bin gives us, of the youthful George Washington
at the frontier town of Martinsburg, West Vir-

ginia, tendering a coonskin in payment of a tavern bill and receiving 158 rabbit skins in change! And we have the picture of Father Duncan, who had seen the Hudson Bay allow the Tsimpsean trappers " two bits in trade " for a marten skin, setting up his own store at Metlakatla and paying two to four dollars for the same grade of pelt. Our Founding Fathers, both east and west, were fur traders.

The explorers—your Cabots and your Berings —cruise along a new coast, poke the noses of their vessels into river mouths and bays, get a general picture, set up a national flag, and sail away to new ports. Then come the fur trader and the trapper, but the trapper stays upon the land, moving ever further back from the sea as settlers come to the coast—for fur traders and settlers play a different game.

Before the Pilgrim Fathers stepped on Plymouth Rock, Captain John Smith was writing of his visit to New England: " Ranging the Coast in a small boat, wee got for trifles neer 1100 Bever skinnes, 100 Martins & neer as many Otters." Beaver became the very symbol of the conquest of our own Northwest and sits to-day upon the crest of Canada, a " totem " reminder of the Hudson Bay men; while Adams says of old New England: " The Bible and the Beaver were the two mainstays of the young colony. The former saved its morals and the latter paid its bills; the rodent's share was a large one!" But Beaver is only one of the fine furs which trappers seek in our Alaskan North to-day.

Muk-pi says that the Raven creator told her people that Beaver would always live along the streams and build strong houses there, and that they too must follow his example. " Beaver will be very cunning, though," the Raven said, " and only clever trappers will ever take him." The Raven first showed Man *Kannukklak,* too, the Muskrat, and told him how to take its skin for warm winter clothing. My own beloved parka, which Muk-pi made, is of the silver muskrat and is trimmed with white reindeer strips and wolverine, with a big wind-ruff of gray wolf to whip across the face and keep your nose and cheeks from freezing.

Beaver and muskrat are half water-animals, depending upon a water catch for food; but the land-fur of Alaska's big trapping spaces is built in good part upon multitudinous red-backed timber mice, field mice of the tundra, lemmings and rabbits. These are vegetarian " sleekit, cow'rin, tim'rous beasties," but of them the larger fur-bearers take daily toll; and the lean and fat years of Alaska's great fur trade have swung in cycles which have been determined by these small and inconsidered animals.

Lemmings are mouse-like things, about five inches long, with stubby tails, fat puffy cheeks, a short head, round small ears, a blunt nose, and digging fore-paws provided with sharp tiny claws. They make toy tunnels under snowbanks in the winter, shallow burrows and galleries in tussocks of turf on the tundra, and spend most of their time there. But if a strong wind comes and blows away the light snow from above these tunnels, after a winter storm they will be seen scurrying about above ground for a time, and this has given rise to a curious tradition among the Eskimos. Their name for white lemming sounds like *kil-yung-mi-tuk,* and means " Belonging-to-the-sky." Muk-pi's people say that these are not earth creatures at all, but sky creatures, blown down to the earth only in stormy weather, whirling round and round in spirals with the snow. And that is why their little tracks are seen only after a storm and why those tracks go always round and round, for they of course are dizzy when they touch the earth! There are no lemmings native to the land, Chick-em will tell you, solemnly. They come down only from above. " We see him come. Your people know, what country he come down from, may-be? "

It's curious how strong this superstition is, and will not down even when you point out to them the little under-snow runways where lemming stays so hidden except in stormy weather. And it's an interesting legend for quite another reason; for I am told that old Norwegians have the same belief, exactly, and the tradition that those excessively numerous hordes of lemmings which at times swarm down from the high lands into their valleys and infest their farms, coming so unexpectedly and in great armies, have " dropped down from the clouds."

The tundra lemming has a silky, gray-brown, soft fur coat which turns an ermine white in polar winter, so that some people call them " white mice of the Arctic." Another type, the tawny lemming or *avwiñu* of the Eskimo, is found in Interior Alaska as well as in the Arctic, and does not turn winter white. Unlike their Northern Europe Lapland cousins, Alaska's lemmings do not, so far as we now know, indulge in those great army-like migrations, lasting sometimes for many months and ending with strange self-destruction as they reach the sea at last and plunge into it. In part upon these Lilliputian pawns of fur—the innumerable fodder of the warring fur world, " restless, pugnacious little animals "—the hierarchy of Alaska's land fur is built. As Stefansson says, " The lemming *implies* the fox!"

Next in order are rabbits, and when rabbits and lemmings both are plentiful, foxes aren't much interested in trap-bait, old-timers say! There is a definitely recognized rabbit cycle, and large numbers die off periodically at intervals of seven to ten years. Tularemia, prevalent among rabbits in the States, may well be that mysterious something which decimates both lemmings and rabbits in Alaska, and this would easily account for the trapper's lean years. I know that Russell Merrill, the Anchorage flier, forced down and without food on a long hike across the tundra, shot and ate a number of lemmings. This brought on a violent case of Rocky Mountain or " deer fly " fever, as tularemia used to be called before people knew what it really was: a plague-like infectious disease occurring in certain rodents, highly fatal to certain groups of animals, and occasionally transmitted to man in a milder form, through handling infected meat or through the bite of insects which carry it. Human death from tularemia is fortunately rare and recovery, though very slow, apparently gives lifelong immunity to man—but *not* to susceptible wild creatures. It's a most curious disease, for different human cases of it may simulate typhoid fever, septic infection, or glanders! To tell the truth, we don't know very much about it, even yet, for it's only since 1920 that tularemia has been recognized and named and definitely pinned down to the mischief of a thing called *Bacterium tularense*—this name being taken from California's Tulare County, where ground-squirrels infected with it were first discovered.

We know, and it's been proved, that snow-shoe and other types of rabbits are especially susceptible to this disease, as well as ground-squirrels, mice, rats, gophers, coyotes, muskrats—and grouse! With such an obvious chain of possible infection between all these neighbor creatures of our wild, both big and little, surely there is at least strong possibility that tularemia may be that secret, swift Something which periodically overtakes certain fur-bearers and has puzzled and mystified our northern trappers for years. It would appear to be one factor, at least, in the very notable drop in Alaska's fox and lynx census, so often noticed by our trappers as following surely on a cut-down bunny population.

Whether or not due to this strange, newly-identified, little-known disease, the fact remains that rabbits do die off or disappear, in roughly seven-to-ten-year cycles. Lynx disappear shortly after the rabbits go, for bunny is their favorite

food, too. This disappearance may be caused
by lowered fecundity or by actual starvation: I
do not know. But trappers say that, in small
rabbit years, lynx is a desperate animal and will
then attack almost anything—even one another
—for food. The fox catch, too, is very seriously
affected whenever those lean years of pestilence
arrive for rabbits and lemmings, to break down
" Nature's social union " of reddened tooth and
claw.

The little ground squirrels or " parkies," as
some call them, which are so common over much
of Alaska, hibernate in winter; but in summer
they feed on various green plants and become
very fat in the fall. Bears are very fond of them
and often you can see a grizzly very busy, digging
some poor ground squirrel out of his hole. These
are the little fellows especially fancied by the
Eskimo for making lighter parkas, and I imagine
that the Eskimo name for them, *sik-sik,* is just
an imitation of their sharp call or chirp. The red
tree squirrel carries a plume. He does not hibernate like sik-sik but has a winter nest often in a
spruce; and sometimes you will find his little
caches packed neatly tight with spruce cones.

The hoary marmot or *sik-sik-puk* (big sik-sik)
is also highly prized for parkas, and enough pelts
to make one coat are called " one skin! " He lives

in rugged mountain places and is a winter sleeper, like the bear, spending the dark months in uninterrupted slumber, living off his fat. Also like the bear, his fur is best if taken in early spring while it is still soft and grayish. Eskimos catch him in traps on his runways, with nooses of whalebone placed in the snow or underground. The women rub and work the skins with their hands to make them very soft—stretch, dry and wash with oil to make them pliable. Thickly built, short eared, with broad and powerful incisors, this " big squirrel " cousin loves to sit upon his hind legs on a little mound in front of his house by day, take a look-see around, whistle and then scamper off if anything startles him. But he'll come back, for he is an inquisitive soul. His fur is much sought, and in the great London fur auctions marmot skins are sold literally by the million.

But the white winter ermine (teréa Eskimos call him, but trappers call him plain weasel!) is much more sought by whites because we think it the truly royal fur. Farther south, where there is little or no snow or deep cold, ermine does not turn dead white in winter; but he is to be found all over Alaska, as far as I know, the heaviest pelts coming from farthest north. He has a lithe, thin, muscular body, is both inquisitive and fearless, and equally at home up in the air in trees, in snow, or underground. Yet fashion takes strange freaks, and even silky pure-white ermine is not respected by this fickle dame. I read in a Paris paper that dyed black ermine is the newest thing on the market! And Lanvin in March of 1930 showed a pink wrap, lined with rabbit dyed pale pink. Surely this is fantasy and enough to make a March hare mad! What would these little northern fur-beasts say, if they could see their precious and protecting winter coat so rainbow-colored?

Mink is a fur the trappers always prize, because it is so lovely in its natural color and because it wears so long and well. Here is another clever canny creature, and Alaska Natives have their countless stories telling of the tricks of mink, raven, wolverine and blue-jay. Fannie Quigley told me of being camped once by a creek and " a mink came out and ate all ten of the grayling I'd cleaned and left, careless, in a basket near the water." Mink can often be caught with rabbit bait, and one friend tells me of a haystack on their place not far from town where they found a mink cache of sixty-seven rabbits, laid up for winter! There's thrift for you. The Innuit use dead-falls and figure-four traps for taking mink, or small wicker fish-traps set in the

creeks under the ice. They say that Mink is a
" small dark man " and he and Raven are great
pals and old companions in cleverness—were
partners and once killed seals together by their
scheming. That's why the Raven will not eat the
flesh of Mink, and they are often seen together
on the tundras. " Him talk about old time,
maybe," was Chick-em's comment.

Marten, too, " live all slame man " in cozy
winter house, so Tinneh say, when he " play card
and make glood eat, all time winter." The
Eskimos account with ease for the strange disappearance of whole species of fur animals by
their own love of gambling games! They say
that in the winter the " owners of the places "
play gambling games with one another and win
from each other large numbers of their local creatures, which then have to go and live upon the
winner's " estate." Fox and lynx prey upon
marten during a dearth of rabbits, and forest fires
take ghastly toll of these tree-loving creatures.
Their food is arctic mice, or birds, eggs, nuts and
berries—a clean and neat and tasty diet, befitting
the possessor of such an exquisite coat.

Seen in a tree, flat upon a branch, you might
imagine Mr. Marten a very large squirrel—for
he has sharp little ears, fat cheeks and a handsome bushy tail. Nothing in fur-land is more

lovely than darkest marten skin or sable, the
product of the darkest coldest forests which tend
to make his pelage extra dark and extra long.
I'm told by fur buyers that, in Siberia, sable
hunting is a fine art, " the most skilful hunters
electing not to trap or shoot the animal, but to
tree it, thus preventing possible injury to the
pelt. When they get an animal treed, they
knock it into a net. Mr. Jaeckel, Mr. Gunther
and Mr. Revillon hold the net!" So, if you
know Fifth Avenue, you will know where all our
good Alaska sables go, when they die.

One of my own very favorite dark northern
furs is wolverine—the favorite too with Eskimos
for lining parka hoods. They say it is the only
fur which will not hold the frost that forms from
breath in very cold weather, and this is a very
important consideration for winter clothing.
Gulo luscus, the glutton, is a growling, blunt-
headed little thief of the Arctic snows and
forests; and though he has a deep, thick, brown-
furred coat that is so strong it simply will not
wear out in a lifetime, yet he is hated by trappers and feared by man and beast. For he is a
lawless robber, and he is devilish strong and
devilish sly. I've heard him called " the lost soul
of a great trapper, devoted to every mischief
that could drive a trapper mad."

Lynx is another handsome northern fur, wearing a thick tawn fallow-gray winter coat, white trimmed, and holding strong steel claws hooked in soft, furry, cat-like pads. Tireless and watchful, he lives on rabbits and on grouse; when these go, Herr Lynx packs his trunk and goes too, evidently, for trappers find him very scarce in the " off " rabbit years. He makes all the cat cries and has all the cat ways but, so far as I know, in spite of his strength he doesn't attack people.

Alaska's foxes are as Joseph-coated as Alaska's bears and, like them, run through pure white into black, with scores of variations in between: Arctic White Fox, which follows in the train of Polar Bear, small, with a woolly underfur that's silky and creamy; his smoky cousin Blue Fox, of that slaty maltese color so desired by fashion and " ranched " upon the southern islands so extensively; Red Fox which varies from pale yellow to dark orange—throat, tip of brush and under-belly white—whose underwool is long and soft, hair plentiful and strong, skin and fur both most durable of all the fox clan; Cross Fox which varies from pale silver-pointed yellow to a deep brown so nearly black that only experts can distinguish it from true black, but wearing always that darkish cross upon his

A SALMON FISHER ON THE YUKON.

Photograph by Merrill, Sitka.

BARÁNOF'S CASTLE, AFTER IT HAD BEEN DESERTED AND ALLOWED TO
FALL TO PIECES.

ALASKAN BEAR CUBS TAKE TO ALASKAN AIR WAYS. LIKE ALL TRUE ALASKANS, THEY WILL "TRY ANYTHING ONCE!"

Photograph by Cann.

MCKINLEY, HIGHEST MOUNTAIN IN THE WORLD ABOVE ITS VALLEY FLOOR.

shoulders, as well as sable socks; Silver or Black
Fox, with top " guard " hairs running black to
silvery, dark upon his shoulders, and whose value
(which can be tremendous) depends upon how
far down his back this black streak runs—
whether a quarter of his length, half, three-
fourths or, in most exceptional cases, *all* the way.
If it does, then he is a true Natural Black Fox,
a very rare thing in the fur world; and you will
pay high for this rarity, if you attempt to buy
his pelage! Foxes are weather prophets and
forecasters, Muk-pi's people say; and when the
first fall foxes caught are lean, old men predict
hard winter.

Those wishing to enwrap their necks in Rey-
nard's pelt, no longer need depend on fur-traps,
though, for a new industry has sprung up in
Alaska and is of great importance to our section
of the world, where *dependably* long cool winters
breed such superior pelage. Fox farming is now
well past the experimental stages and all along
the southern coast and out on the Aleutian chain,
a small island is either leased from Uncle Sam
for this purpose or " squatted." If it contains
fifty acres, it will very likely be stocked with ten
pairs of foxes, which are turned loose and allowed
to roam at large over the entire island, choosing
their own mates and making their own dens. It

is not at all uncommon for blue fox vixens to have fifteen puppies, but seven would be a good average, I believe.

In the earliest days of this fox industry, the animals were left to forage for themselves; but now practically all ranchers feed their foxes a good clean ration of fish from the salmon, cod, halibut, rockfish, skates and herring all so plentiful nearabout, or hair-seal, porpoise and white-whale meat, when these can be obtained. Regular feeding makes these animals quite tame, and this proves a great advantage: when they are wanted, they can be taken in the feeding pens, and so there is no need to use a steel contraption.

Mink, too, are being ranched all over Alaska; at Bethel on the Kuskokwim, Petersburg down on the Southeast Coast, Shaw Creek, Berry's Landing, and at the Taku Farm on Glacier Highway near Juneau. The Laughlin Brothers from this last locality recently sent thirty of their live mink to Sweden, to start a mink ranch there, and these sold for $324 a pair! Indeed, it's not at all unusual for mink farmers to have their entire stock of kittens contracted for, long before whelping time. The number of mink kittens in a litter will sometimes run as high as ten, but "we are seven" is the average young mink family, too.

It seems to me that our English language has no more appealing forthright narrative, for frontier-minded people, than doughty Captain John Smith's *Description of New-England,* written at the end of the greatest exploratory century our world has ever known and at the beginning of the most widely colonizing era of history. It proved a guide-book full of information for those who ventured over-seas to settle in America. After severing connection with the Jamestown colony, of which he had been president in 1608, Captain Smith made another voyage further north, under an engagement with London merchants, to fish for cod, barter for furs, and explore the country for settlement. It was he who, at the request of Prince Charles you will remember, named this new country he explored " New-England." His story starts: " In the moneth of Aprill 1614 with 2 Ships from London of a few Marchants I chanced to arriue in New-England, a parte of Ameryca, at the Ile of Monahiggan, in 40 1/2 of Northeasterly latitude: our plot was there to take Wales & make tryalls of a Myne of Gold & Copper. If these failed, Fish & Furres was then our refuge."

All this has a most familiar ring to Alaskan pioneers, and for that matter, " Fish & Furres " have proved our own refuge more than once in

Alaska's history, when " Mynes of Gold & Copper " somehow failed to materialize! Prosaic export statistics prove that, in spite of numerous gold stampedes, we in Alaska can say to-day exactly what the early settlers at Cape Ann once frankly admitted: " Our main ende hath been Fish! " Yet I have not spared much space here to speak about Alaska's fish, for that's not necessary. Alaska's fish advertise themselves. With more than two-thirds of the world's total canned salmon coming yearly from Alaska, with Alaska packing last year over five million cases of salmon alone, there is scarcely a person in the civilized world to-day who does not know Alaska as the greatest of salmon lands. With every home in America familiar with those tall red cans of the Alaska salmon pack, why add to that story? Millions of people who have never for a moment dreamed that Alaska's population is half white colonists, their kinsmen—who think that all Alaska's Natives are igloo Eskimos and all its climate icebergs and glaciers—are now eating those quarter-billion cans of salmon we packed last year: cans which, placed end to end, would stretch out more than *nineteen thousand miles!*

Salmon spawn in more than a thousand of Alaska's streams, and have always been a main food for Haida and Thlingit, Tinneh Indians,

Aleutians and Eskimos alike.   The shining silver
fish, with moss-green back and bright red flank,
stirs the jade water into silver at the spawning
time, leaping homeward by the hundred thousand to those very streams where they were born.
On the Yukon, all the summer months are dated
by the salmon runs, and Tinneh say: " It was
after the run of the dog-salmon, and while the
summer-salmon were running," to place the time
of a story.   For theirs is yet another calendar
having the mark of beasts and fishes for its signs
of Zodiak!   Add halibut fisheries on the coast;
add shrimp and herring, cod, snapper, crabs—
and here's a source of vitamines and iodine, seemingly inexhaustible.   For where the icy Arctic
waters meet the warm currents sweeping from
the southern seas, there will be the richest fisheries of the world—about Iceland, Newfoundland, and Norway as well as here about the shores
of our own Uncle Sam's Alaska.

XVII

Baránof Builds His Castle

Come, my tan-faced children.
Follow well in order, get your weapons ready.
Have you your pistols? Have you your sharp-edged
 axes?
> Pioneers! O pioneers!

For we cannot tarry here.
We must march, my darlings, we must bear the brunt of
 danger—
We, the youthful sinewy races—all the rest on us depend.
> Pioneers! O pioneers!

We, detachments steady throwing,
Down the edges, through the passes, up the mountains
 steep—
Conquering, holding, daring, venturing, as we go the
 unknown ways.
> Pioneers! O pioneers!

WHITMAN.

IF you should travel round the world from east
 to west, and some friend of yours should
travel round the world from west to east, you'd
cross a spot out in Alaska's Aleutian Islands
where the days change shift and you can watch
yesterday, to-day and to-morrow all meeting

there, at the International Date Line. A hidden
truth as well as obvious fact lies here; for out on
those Aleutians which stretch like hooves of rearing horse to strike almost to Asia, Alaska's past,
present and future do come together, as no other
where.

Although a young thing yet, and cub of the
Great Bear, Alaska has a story that is already
grave, noble, and in many ways tragic, for it is
a land not only of the far away but also of the
long ago. The story begins like Macbeth's battle
on the blasted heath. " Prophecy hovers round.
Horns are heard blowing in the mist, and a con-
fused uproar of savage tumult and outrage. We
catch glimpses of giant figures—mostly warriors
at strife. But there are ploughmen, too, it seems,
breaking the primeval clod, and we hear the
sound of forests crashing to the axe. Around all
is the lap of waves and the cry of seamen beach-
ing their ships."

It is not only a topsy but a turvy story, for the
first chapter of Alaska's finding was not written
in the court of Ferdinand and Isabella, nor yet
upon the painted beaks of Northmen's ships, but
in the thirty-five scrolled letters of the old Russian alphabet, so full of " shtchah " and " cheh."
A caressive language, full of diminutives and
" little inconsequential syllables, thrown in like

talking to a baby," Max Eastman calls it. He adds: " And there is nothing less like a Russian than an American!" So that is why this naked bawling babyhood of our Alaska seems such a foreign far-off thing, to us Americans. Alaska's baby years in history were wholly Russian, and Russia is, as Pushkin said, " like a lawless comet in the calculated round of stars."

In the same spacious years when Francis Drake was sailing westward round the globe, free-booting for Queen Elizabeth, the singular Cossack people of Russia—" brave as Spaniards, tough as gipsies "—began to push out eastward from the Caspian and Black Seas, in a century-march which took them finally to Siberia, the Russian Canaan. Riding tough ponies, as adequate to long hard marches as their masters and as equal to all cold, hunger, and fatigue, they drew out from the Volga and across the Urals in a curious sable-hunt of discovery as well as conquest which led in time half round the world— traveling in a broad stream straight across the vast plains of Siberia, in a line equally distant from the mountains of the South and the tundras of the North. Their broken bridle-trail was in a later day to become one of the world's truly great inland highways, and where the Cossacks stopped for a moment in that march they built a fort or ostrog in the wilderness, which later would become a city.

Fierce and cunning Cossacks—always astride tough horseflesh which could scrape the winter snows like reindeer for their nourishment or, if grass was scarce, eat frozen fish with relish—first reached the Lena River in 1628, ten men against the disunited semi-nomad ten thousand people of that great valley, busy training deer, hunting with their half-wild dogs, or fighting one another with a primitive bow and lance. Buta reached the Yana in 1638—when Jacques Marquette, who was to make our Mississippi known, was yet a year-old baby in Laon, France—and by the next winter, these onward-pushing Cossacks had an ostrog built at Okhotsk on our western ocean, at the narrowing top of the Pacific. The pelts of precious little sables had been the bait which drew them, for sable then as now was fur for kings. These wild *promyshleniki,* free-booting hunters on their own account and risk, found furs a currency of Empire.

When Cossacks reached the coast, they soon began to pick up rumors of a land beyond. What did it mean, there in Kamchatka, when tall tree trunks that never grew in Asia were thrown up on the beach? When flocks of land-birds flew in from the East? When whales were cast up on the shore with spear-heads of a strange design caught in their flanks? As *promyshleniki* wandered up along the coast in trade, and made a contact with the warlike Chuk-chee, they noticed shrewdly that the waves which broke here did not bear as long a swell as those that broke on Asia further south. Often, in fights with Chuk-chee, Russians took a captive who spoke another speech and wore a button made of ivory thrust through his lips and cheek. What was that Bolshaia Zemblia, that great land lying somewhere to the East? Questioned, the Chuk-chee said that in the summertime they paddled to it, in winter by swift reindeer team they drove to it "in one day, on the ice." All this, reported at the court of Pieterburgh (Saint Petersburg or Petrograd or Leningrad, as years have brought their changing word-fashions!) caused fascinated interest in the mind of a certain ruler, whose bold decisions had a way of starting epochs.

Peter was truly The Great. It was he whose dreaming and fanatical eyes, even when old and blood-shot with a madman's orgies, turned now toward the East and, sea-and-sailor wise that he was, made ukase: " You are to go to Kamchatka and farther, as you have been ordered, and *determine whether Asia and America are united; and go not only north and south but east and west,*

and put on a chart all that you see." Gargan-
tua, colossal drunkard, yet he had made already
possible the Great Russia, the Holy Russia, of a
later century. He had taken the monstrous
sleeping Bear with bloody claws and, as Herbert
Gorman says, " turned its mystical and savage
face toward Europe, awakened it to the pulse of
modern time, created for it a navy and an army
and a centralized government. He was a great
experimenter, a great innovator, a force courageous enough to open the way to an intelligent
Westernization of the Russias, in spite of the
obsessive desire for isolation that permeated the
Princes and the Bishops of the steppes. . . .
Surrounded by his slaves, his grotesque dwarfs,
his mock-Pope and his burlesque religious orgies,
he was manifestly a madman; yet there was another side to him, the side that reveals him as a
prophetic and far-sighted statesman."

Though Peter's days were numbered, the impatient autocrat determined to send out an expedition commanded by competent naval officers,
accompanied by a corps of scientists, to settle
beyond question whether it really was the West
Coast of America which faced Siberia and Kamchatka. Boldly conceiving an American Russia,
as he already held a European and an Asiatic
Russia, with his own hand, although a dying

man, early in January of 1725 he drew up instructions for this voyage and himself selected Vitus Bering, Martin Spangenburg, Alexei Chirikof, for leaders. " Now that the country is in no danger from enemies," he said to Count Apraxin, " we should strive to win for her glory along the lines of Arts and Science. I have written out these instructions, and on account of my health I entrust the execution of them, point by point, to you, Fedor Matveevich."

Peter the Great died later in that same January, so that the final organization of his perfected plan fell to a Lithuanian farmer's girl named Catherine, his wife, who had the wit to rule as the first Empress of Russia. Eight days after Peter's death she handed Peter's final instructions to Captain Bering, and on that very day he set out over the long Siberian trail, to overtake his party which had already started Eastward. After unusual delay and almost insurmountable hardship, this First Kamchatka Expedition did advance northward to those Straits which now bear Bering's name, and did determine that Asia and the Great Land to the eastward came close together there *but did not touch*. Then a Second Kamchatka Expedition was fitted out, also under Captain Bering, and this proved quite the most brilliant effort toward

scientific discovery which any government had
ever made, up to that time.   Because of the distance and the difficulty, every salary was doubled
for those engaged and, though the expedition
took six years to cross Siberia with supplies, and
though meanwhiles the Imperial Treasurer
groaned at the expense, on June 4 of the year
1741 (during that summer when a certain hot and
fiery young debater, Sam Adams, was working
for a Master's Degree at Harvard, and small John
Adams was a boy not yet six) two boats that had
been built at Okhotsk finally set sail from Avatcha
Bay and on July 15 America was sighted—a
wooded island almost due west of Metlakatla.

The century-march of swarming *promyshleniki,* which had crossed the vast continent of
Asia, now pushed on across the narrowed Pacific to the fire-breathing islands, topless peaks
and cedar-forested coast of our Alaska. To some
Americans, Alaska is Siberian; but to Siberians,
Alaska *was* America. Bering's crew had
brought back precious sea-otter pelts from the
Aleutians, and *promyshleniki* who had braved
Siberia were just as ready now to brave these
treacherous northern waters, for the sable was
as nothing in value when compared with this
amphibious otter, which now lured those venturesome dare-devils on and out among the little

islands and the fogs of northern winters. The
same cunning bravery which had won Siberia for
the Tsar, made helpless here the mild and Eski-
moan islanders. Aleut and Indian ways alike
began to change with the first coming of the Russians, just as Russian ways were to change later
with the coming of gold-seeking argonauts, and
the ways of ninety-eight were to change with the
later coming of roads, railroads, automobiles and
airplanes.

Alaska was discovered by a Dane in the service
of Russia and not by a Genoese in the service of
Spain: from across the Pacific at Avatcha Bay
and not from the Atlantic and the Port of Palos:
was possessed for Empress Elizaveta and not for
Queen Isabella: in 1741 and not in 1492. This
makes Alaska young. It also makes Alaska different.

What the Russians did, after their coming, and
how they laid here the foundations of an empire,
in colony and trade, I have told elsewhere.*
Merely to see was to covet those sea-otter skins,
and it's small wonder that the Russians were led
on by *morskie bobri,* so duskily soft in rich dark

* *Uncle Sam's Attic* is the story Mary Lee Davis has told of the
Bear Cub's growing up, with intimate details from her own
Alaskan life of all the many present-day activities and ventures
now going on in Uncle Sam's North, of which so few Americans
have first-hand knowledge.

fur and yet so glowing and so splendent.   The
Chinese, too, were covetous of these glorious
peltries, and even as long ago as the mid-eight-
eenth century were paying eighty to a hundred
rubles for one skin; for sea otters were then the
most valuable fur in all the world. Eskimos and
Aleuts had traded in furs long before the advent
of Europeans, and oceanic mammals that blow
or lift their velvet-black heads near Muk-pi's
country had long been sought, while the Yukon
tribes lived in a land famous for its soft-furred
animals, whose pelts they traded in every direction. But the Russians here, as Hudson Bay
men in our nearer Northwest, now stimulated the
fur-trade to the utmost and taught new means
of capture, including the use of firearms, so that
within a century the lovely sea otter became
almost extinct and very few men now living have
ever seen one on those kelpy reefs where once
they used to be so very plentiful. The court of
Catherine the Great was satisfied with tribute in
furs,—taxes could be paid in furs; and, as at
Jamestown from 1607 onward, so now at Kodiak
and Sitka in the late eighteenth and early nineteenth century—though colonists might be in
actual need of food, The Company demanded:
gold and cedar there, sea otter and the fur seal
here. Famine and hardship, Indian torch and

hatred, might stalk the near-by woods; but Empire must be served, and raw materials of commerce be shipped back home.

In their beginnings, those early small American colonies upon the eastern coast were largely business ventures, organized by groups of individuals and joint-stock companies and, as such, " but episodes in the expansion of English commerce." So our Alaska began its history, too, as but an episode in the expanding commercial empire of the Tsars, and grew to early cub-hood as but an episode in the expanding American commercial empire. For long years Russian-America was merely " The Fur Country," as were also Northwestern U. S. A. and Canada's Northwest, in their young day. Although the Russians were cruel, what did it matter if Aleuts died by thousands—from bullet wound, from porridge seasoned with corrosive sublimate, from rape, plunder, wholesale murder—so long as dividends went regularly home, to shareholders in the great Russian-American Fur Company?

True, the outrages of the *promyshleniki* were not known in Russia for many years; and what difference would it have made, if they had been known? The Tsar Paul was a lunatic and they murdered him, but meanwhiles he had signed the ukase giving Shelikof's Fur Company the same

practically unlimited powers of life and death
and empire which the Hudson Bay Company
once held in Canada. Tsar Alexander I his son
was not so bad or silly; but even he was " not the
man his grandmother was "—Great Catherine
II, who died in 1796 and under whose long reign
the empire of fur was so extended. Great Catherine had a fancy that sea-otter fur became her
demi-Holstein beauty, so sea otter were hunted
up and down Alaska's coast with fury and with
frenzy. The Russians did not purchase skins,
but had the animals killed by Aleut hunters
whom they had virtually enslaved; and, as time
passed, the social chasm dividing " savage " and
" civilized " was gradually filled with creoles, the
Native ascending somewhat in the scale, the Russian descending.

The Aleuts were " converted " to the Ortho-
dox Greek Church, but most of this imposed religion extended very little above their knees,
while up to 1868 there was small trace of Christian teaching among the Thlingit or the Eskimos.
Meares noticed that wherever Russians settled,
the Natives were forbidden to keep canoes larger
than would carry two men, and large sea-lion-
skin bidars (as the Russians called the Eskimo-
like umiaks of the Aleuts, and which the Natives
used for war-canoes or the removal of whole

families or villages) were seized by Russians for
their own use, just as fast as Natives built them.
What business had these "savages," either to
war or visit? Their business was to lead a life
of unwilling, unrelieved, and slave-like industry,
getting out furs of sea otter for Catherine the
Great of Russia.

The Hudson Bay Company, who penetrated
to upper Yukon posts by 1839, were hard task-
masters, too, and thrifty bargainers as well.
They used to sell their cheap flint-lock muskets
to the Indians by standing the gun upright and
then piling marten skins beside it, until they
evened the top of the gun barrel—and it is said
the factor had a very heavy hand! But Veniami-
nof tells how one Russian on the South Coast
" experimented " with the penetrating power of
musket balls by " tying twelve Aleuts together
and discharging his rifle at them, at close range.
It is reported that the bullet lodged in the *ninth
man.*" The Russians spread the circle of their
power by building forts at river mouths, and
some of these are still standing, so stockily were
they made.—In 1833, one Patrick Shirreff visited
a little hamlet of 150 log houses on Lake Michi-
gan—named slightingly with an Ojibway word
Chicago, " wild onion place "—and found a big
pow-wow of Pottawatomie Indians going on,

" forests and prairies in the neighborhood studded with the tents of the Indians and numerous herds of horses browsing in all directions." In that same year the Russians reached the Yukon's mouth and built a fort there.

What Clive was to India, what Cecil Rhodes was to South Africa—something of that and something more Baránof was to Russian America. One man, at some strategic point or period, is sometimes able to give a push to the slow roll of history which turns a hazy dream of empire into fact, by the sheer quality of his character. Looking back, we can see now that the whole course of our American Revolution was probably determined, when Washington decided to risk his dear-loved, peaceful Virginia plantation and cast in his lot with " a pack of rebels, 'gainst the Crown." The future of Alaska was determined when Shelikof sought out this Russian trader-man Baránof and persuaded him to take charge of affairs in Russian America. Sitka and Kodiak were much further from St. Petersburg than Boston and Charleston were from London, and Baránof dealt—as other colonial administrators have dealt—with a mysterious, far-off, semi-divine Government to whom colonial affairs were often misrepresented by designing and unscrupulous officials and meddlers.

Alexander Andreïvitch Baránof was a Slav, born at Kargapol in the very year when Washington left school to do surveying for Lord Fairfax. Unlike Washington, however, Baránof was an insignificant-looking person, small in stature, with scant red hair and yellowed complexion, but with unusually shrewd eyes and a most kindly and soft voice—when unaroused. The British and " Boston men " who used to put in often at Old Sitka, to trade there and repair their vessels on those ship-ways which Baránof built, called him " the grizzled bear," after those trading *prosnics* when they clinked cans with him in "maudlin mixture of punch and peltry." They often told of the raw rum and boiling punch he drank, " strong as sulphur," and that he would not deal with any " cold water caitiff "! This was a part of his " system "; for Baránof knew that Baránof drunk was more than equal to the others, drunk or sober, in any dicker. Deliberately cultivating a most rowdy atmosphere, when dealing with " the trade," Baránof showed the other side of him both in his warm-felt love of music (and like King Cole, his call for pipe and bowl meant always fiddlers three, as well!) and in his warm and deep affection for his daughter, for whose instruction and companionship he had imported a matronly German governess. Even

when in later life he became, as he called himself, " a person worn out with hardship and
fatigue, and with a temper soured by adversity "
—though sick and tired and sometimes cross—
his daughter's fingers touching the piano keys
would soothe the grizzled bear to peaceful dreaming.

He was a man of dreams, of mighty dreams.
Khlebnikof said of him: " He was never at his
wits' end and never faint-hearted. . . . During
the whole term of his administration he exhibited
a rare disinterestedness, and though he had every
chance of enriching himself, had never taken advantage of his positoin. Even when seventy, life
and energy sparkled in his eye; and there are not
a few now living in the Colonies, whom he helped
out in difficulty." For nearly thirty years Baránof served his Company and Country on this far
coast, raised towns and villages, built fleets of
seagoing ships, traded vigorously with California, Hawaii and Canton, with Hudson Bay men
and " the republicans of Boston and America,"
as he called us. He won the deeply genuine respect and the true friendship of that elegant and
cultured courtier, Rezanof—scientist, linguist,
diplomat, statesman, one of ten Barons of the
Russian Empire, Chamberlain of the Russian
Court, intimate of Tsars—who wintered with him

once, at Sitka. He dug here the foundations and laid the sills on which the empire-builders of the future were to rear dominion, power and glory. Ever and always he worked night and day to hold this land for his own people, against the British, Spanish, Swedish, and John Jacob Astor's Yankee outpost on the Columbia.

He wrote back home a letter, once, containing a noteworthy mixture of piety, business and patriotism, which fits as the unlocking key to his peculiar temper. He hoped, he said, " That the fruits of the discoveries of Russian navigators may not be enjoyed by European or other Companies, depriving us of our hard-earned advantages. I trust that God in His justice will allow us to enjoy the fruits of our enterprise, and as, with His help, I, an ignorant subject, have been able to add something to the vast dominion of his Imperial Majesty, we must hope that we shall find the means to preserve our new possessions intact, and make them profitable."

Those who knew him best and longest declared that Baránof was neither cruel nor vindictive, as enemies reported. He proved quite brave and strong enough to control even the lawless Cossack *promyshleniki,* and was at heart always a Slav, with all the cunning of his race. But he was capable of heights of loyalty unequaled in

his time, among his own people; and when at
long last he was called back home to face the
jealous plots of enemies and give accounting of
his stewardship, he died of broken heart to leave
his North, and waters of the Straits of Sunda
closed upon his tired-out body.   Contemporaries
spoke of him as one who had kept faith with all
the best traditions of his time and, under unex-
ampled tempting, never knew avarice, hoarded
riches, nor played false with his word or friend—
" with all his faults, which were neither few nor
small."

It was Baránof (who himself was quite con-
tent to live here first in a small ochre-daubed log
hut which leaked both summer and winter) at
whose word the sound of Russian axes rang
against the slopes of Verstovoi, at whose command the fort at Sitka rose upon a rock—and
was consecrated to the Archangel Michael—" in
the hope that this great champion of the Lord
would protect our promyshleniki."   With his
strong sea-glass and his sharp keen eyes, he swept
the forest and this lovely Sitka harbor, which he
himself had chosen as the fitting seat of empire
in the North.   Upon this chosen rock, princely
successors were to raise " Baránof's Castle," as
it was always called—a notable structure of mast
timber, hand-hewn logs boarded over, which

dominated the archangelic village until, one early morning back in 1894, the great pile burned to nothing. Maybe it is a symbol—that Baránof never saw Baránof's Castle, the finest fruit of his own building. Maybe it is a symbol, too, that on this spot to-day our Uncle Sam has built an agricultural station, in promise of the fuller flowering of Alaska's future.

The Thlingit who lived near here could not be induced to trade with Russians nor to work for them, and so Aleutians in great numbers were imported from The Westward and in their skin bidarkas hunted sea otter upon Alexander Archipelago, the California coast, and sometimes even as far south as Santa Barbara Islands. In the year when France made Bonaparte a consul for life, the Thlingit burned Baránof's first Sitkan fort, but it didn't *stay* burned any more than Bonaparte " stayed put " as Consul! Baránof rebuilt his fort, stronger and better. He made ploughs at his foundry here, and shipped them down to California; and half the missions there listened to bells cast here, in Sitka's foundry. Though truly religious, in his way, Baránof did not always get along well with the priests sent out from Russia to augment his colonies. A stupendous worker himself, he wanted to see work done; and the Russian Church had 180 holi-

days in each year! Of course, no one would think
of working on a church holiday, and it's a marvel
how Baránof—so far from everything and shaping a colonial power with his two naked hands—
ever accomplished what he did.

A visiting sea captain tells of a dinner with
Baránof, to which he was invited together with
his officers and the commanders of several
American vessels then in port. " The fort . . .
consisted of strong wooden bastions and palisades. The houses, barrack magazines, and
manager's residence were built of exceedingly
thick logs. In Baránof's house the furniture and
finishing were of fine workmanship and very
costly, having been brought from St. Petersburg
and England; but what astonished me most was
the large library in nearly all European languages and the collection of fine paintings—this
in a country where probably only Baránof can
appreciate a picture and no travelers are apt to
call except the skippers of American trading vessels . . . Mr. Baránof treated us to an excellent dinner, during which we had music."

Baránof, patriot and trader, was a poet too.
Upon the founding of Fort New Archangel on
Sitka Bay in 1799, he composed an ode which his
wild *promyshleniki* chanted in rough chorus on
that occasion. He knew so well the words to

lift their hearts and bind their loyalties! Here
it is*—a ringing song of conscious empire-build-
ing, turning the homesickness of rough and
lonely men into a dreamer's aspiration, making a
glory out of every hardship:

The Russian mind, to commerce prone,
A people free o'er seas has thrown—
Far lands to seek, fresh vantage win
For Sovereign and for kith and kin.
 All-powerful God has lent His grace
 Russia's high hardihood to brace;
 Scarce glimpsed as yet, this spacious coast
 Anon a sturdy folk shall boast.
No pompous Grecian muse we crave
To sing this Union of the Brave!
Our charter this: Learn Nature's laws;
Live downright lives; hold the good cause!
 Let dwellings crown our new-born land.
 Russia aspires!—See Nootka stand.
 Rude tribes and Nature wild are tamed
 And friendship's blithesome sway proclaimed.

Illustrious Peter, couldst but thou—
Vast, prescient soul—awaken now,
What joys were thine to view this spoil,
The first-fruits of thy children's toil!

 Lured by a Golden Fleece, of yore
 The Argonauts sought alien shore.
 Had they but gained *this* teeming strand,
 How blest had been their Fatherland!

* AUTHOR'S NOTE: For this English version I am indebted to
R. H. Geoghegan of Fairbanks, who translated it for us from the
March, 1849, number of the magazine *Moskvitjanin*.

Yet, though no aureate pelt *our* guide,
Gold flows to us from every side—
The guerdon gallant ventures win.
—Take heed lest stranger " friends " thrust in!
    Suharev's Tower, the lordly Bell,
    The Tsar-of-Cannon—hear Moscow tell.
    Marvels like these, or Great Iván,
    For *us* are naught. *Our* pride is Man!
To Glory led, in Honor reared,
By labors of our comrades cheered,
Wide spread we our Colonial bounds—
So all to Russia's fame redounds.
    Should any mourn his plight forlorn,
    Laugh we such narrow cares to scorn!
    For Russia's weal 'tis *well* to dwell
    'Mong regions stern, 'mid tribesmen fell.
A dauntless, hardy troop we stand,
'Neath midnight sun, on unworn land.
In friendship firm, dire in the fray,
Lift up your hearts!—" Russia for aye! "
    We little reck of pelf or show,
    Share brethren's mirth, lighten their woe.
    —If toward our Goal we speeded well,
    Let patriots of the morrow tell.

There are many islands in the great semi-circle curve of the bay at Sitka, ringed by umber seaweed at low tide. The town lies in the same latitude as Balmoral, where there is yet another famous castle! But the Japan Current sweeping in here makes this a soft climate, full of clear luminous light on fine days; and during all the years the Russians kept a weather station on

Japonski Island, out in Sitka harbor, the mercury hit zero only four times. This bay has often been compared to the Bay of Naples—surpassing it, some think, in beauty. Mount Edgecumbe (named by famous Captain James Cook) rears a snow-filled crater high above it, and Edgecumbe's slopes are bluer than lapis lazuli.

The heavy castle crowned a rocky headland about a hundred feet above the town, where formerly the Thlingit had a fort; but the rest of the settlement lay upon the bay and at the base of that green pyramid which is Mount Verstovoi. The fort held fifty cannon, in the old days, and the gate in the stockade leading into the Indian village was always closed at nights, while watchmen cried the hours. The " Castle " was a far finer residence than any early English colonial governor knew, upon our eastern shores. A hundred and forty feet long and seventy wide, built of heavy cedar logs, the walls were pierced with copper bolts that held them firmly to the rock with rivets. Baránof's castle was a Russian symbol, and must not be cast down. On a rough exterior scale and yet not lacking in some architectural touch of grace, it wore a ship-walk on its top like old sea-captains' homes back in Nantucket, commanding harbor view and first sight of returning ships. Down in the village were a hundred and fifty solid wooden houses, with whitewashed walls now lichen stained and weather beaten, their once red roofs now heavy with moss. But formerly this moss-grown Sitka was a busy place and did a trade that stretched all up and down the Pacific, bartered with Yankee and British ship masters. Sir George Simpson tells that when he visited Sitka there were " excellent tradesmen, engineers, armorers, tinsmiths, cabinet-makers, jewellers, watch-makers, tailors, cobblers, builders," and Sitka had a foundry, a sawmill, and for many years the most complete shipyard on the north Pacific coast, where vessels of all nations put in for repairs.

Salaries of the Fur Company's officers ran from three to twelve thousand rubles a year, and they were provided besides with firewood, candles, house and servant. At all seasons of the year their tables were supplied with venison, fowl, vegetables, berries and fish. There were about 1,200 men here with their families in 1840, and some 500 troops. The Company and Naval officers stationed here had a club-house back of the old Cathedral, which held a library of 2,000 books and 400 periodicals, as well as a valuable collection of charts and was provided with billiard, and card rooms. Sitkans had a tea garden, a race course, and a promenade with

graveled walk that ran along that lovely curve
of beach and back through heart of primitive
woods to the banks of Indian River, where little
rustic bridges had been built over the clear
stream. High ferns ran riot here, then as to-
day, and mosses covered every fallen log with
velvet carpet. White clover blew its drifts of
blossom beside the spruce walks and the cedar
forest clearings, salmonberries and wild roses
tangled upon the hill slopes, and tiny humming
birds and great black ravens were symbols,
maybe, in the eyes of beautiful Princess Maksoutoff (who walked here often and so loved these
woodsy ways) of all that contradictory twin-
souled Russia which she had left so far behind
in this new world. It was she who wept, with
unabashed abandon, watching her Russian flag
catch in its final downfall, that sad and rainy
Sitka day in '67; and she—most noble and also
most gracious of them all—was the most long remembered afterward, for her dear tact and
charm.

Yet Princess Maksoutoff was only one of
many notable chatelaines who came to Baránof's
Castle—such as Baron Wrangell's wife, or
Madame Kupreanof who had crossed all Siberia
with her husband, on horseback back in 1835, to
reach the new colony. Russian-American gov-

ernors were usually drawn from the very highest ranks and noblest families in the naval service, and visiting democratic Yankee skippers were rather overawed to find here, at Baránof's Castle, a miniature court composed of captains courageous, counts, barons, and even princes of the royal blood, entertaining royally. State dinners were given by the governor each Sunday after service, the officers attending in full dress with blazing decorations; there was a constant round of balls, the nights were filled with music floating down from the high castle rock, and card parties and amateur theatricals were favorite amusements. "Russian hospitality is proverbial," visiting Whymper wrote, "and we all suffered somewhat from it. The first phrase of their language acquired by us was *petnatchit copla,* fifteen drops! . . . Memory refuses to retain the number of times we had to drink tea."

In 1842, when Charles Dickens was touring America and finding our manners execrable, our grammar "more than doubtful," our speech "the oddest vulgarisms," our roads impassable, our bedrooms "always uncomfortable," Sir George Simpson was making a trip round the world. He stopped at Sitka for a visit, and wrote on leaving: "The farewell dinner, to which about thirty of us sat down, exceeded in sumptuousness anything that I had yet seen, even at the same hospitable board. The glass, the plate, and the appointments in general were very costly; the viands were excellent; and Governor Etholin played the part of host to perfection." The governors brought out all their house furnishings from Russia, there was luxury here as well as comfort, the castle was richly furnished, the drawing-room a miniature Versailles Hall of Mirrors. The big brass samovar was always boiling there, and choicest " caravan tea," pungent and bracing, the welcome brew for all comers. Some, like Sir Edward Belcher, spoke most admiringly of the fine caviar and potent punches served here!

Baránof's Castle has fallen, and in its place is now a farm building. The massive wrought brass chandeliers, the giant porcelain stoves in corners of its great rooms—stoves which ate up whole forests—the lantern and reflector from the castle tower which once was harbor beacon, the delicately carved railing about the little boudoir in the fine drawing-room, the billiard room where princes played by branching candle light, the ballroom where they danced to sound of throbbing inlaid old guitars of sweetly melancholy tone and where strange Russian love songs once were sung—all these are gone. Saint Michael's

Church still stands, a century old, green roof and
bulging carrot-shaped spire telling of olden days;
and chimes sent long ago from Moscow still ring
the hours. It faces down the old main street of
Sitka to that harbor, with commanding view, and
is still crammed with gems of semi-oriental,
Byzantine, exquisite treasure, though glory has
departed even here. For change of ways came
with the going of the Russians, that day in '67,
and even Sunday changed. Once it came eastward from a Holy Moscow, but the American
Sabbath came traveling westward and so it fell
upon a different day entirely. Even the very
year was lost, when the old Julian calendar was
superseded by the strange new ways that Boston
men were bringing.

Then Russia's Bear got into strangle-grips
with Britain's Lion, down there in the Crimea.
Later, in hurt and brittle pride, a Russian Tsar
did Uncle Sam a favor, just to spite England.
Still later, fearing that in yet another Crimea
his too-far-distant colony in America might be
snatched from him, Great Catherine's great-
grandson offered Alaska to us, for next to nothing, only to take it off his hands and keep his
enemy from grabbing it. We did, though grudg-
ingly, and mainly on account of that past favor,
unforgotten. That's how the Cub of the Great

Bear came to live in Uncle Sam's attic—an attic full of unexpected golden dust and many a yet unopened treasure-chest. We who live in Alaska are now busy opening those treasure-chests, and finding riches Peter never guessed and shrewd Baránof never dreamed, for all his keen far-sighted eyes.

So much undreamed has come, what more is coming—to our American Alaska? Poets are seers, and perhaps a poet sees it:

" I chant the world on my Western Sea;
  I chant, copious, the islands beyond, thick as stars in
    the sky;
  I chant the new empire, grander than any before, as
    in a vision it comes to me;
  I chant America the mistress; I chant a greater su-
    premacy;
  I chant, perfected, a thousand blooming cities yet in
    time, on those groups of sea-islands—
My sail-ships and steam-ships threading the archi-
    pelagoes,
My stars and stripes fluttering in the wind. . . .

Were the children straying . . . were the precedent
    dim ages debouching . . .
Were the centuries steadily footing it that way, all
    the while unknown—for you, for reasons?
They are justified, they are accomplished."

*   *   *